my **revision** notes

OCR (A) GCSE
SCHOOLS HISTORY PROJECT

Louise O'Gorman

Editor: Bill Marriott

HODDER
EDUCATION
AN HACHETTE UK COMPANY

Photo credits

p.35 © Hulton Archive/Getty Images; **p.39** © The British Library/HIP/TopFoto; **p.55** © MARTIN BOND/SCIENCE PHOTO LIBRARY; **p.61** © Bettmann/Corbis; **p.66** © Punch Limited/TopFoto; **p.68** © Punch Limited/TopFoto; **p.79** © 2005 Roger-Viollet/TopFoto; **p.101** © Across the Continent: 'Westward the Course of Empire takes its way', 1868, (litho), Currier, N. (1813–88) and Ives, J.M. (1824–95)/Private Collection/The Bridgeman Art Library; **p.113** © The Granger Collection, NYC/TopFoto; **p.124** © World History Archive/TopFoto.

Every effort has been made to trace all copyright holders, but if any have been inadvertently overlooked the Publishers will be pleased to make the necessary arrangements at the first opportunity.

Although every effort has been made to ensure that website addresses are correct at time of going to press, Hodder Education cannot be held responsible for the content of any website mentioned in this book. It is sometimes possible to find a relocated web page by typing in the address of the home page for a website in the URL window of your browser.

Hachette UK's policy is to use papers that are natural, renewable and recyclable products and made from wood grown in sustainable forests. The logging and manufacturing processes are expected to conform to the environmental regulations of the country of origin.

Orders: please contact Bookpoint Ltd, 130 Milton Park, Abingdon, Oxon OX14 4SB. Telephone: +44 (0)1235 827720. Fax: +44 (0)1235 400454. Lines are open 9.00a.m.–5.00p.m., Monday to Saturday, with a 24-hour message answering service. Visit our website at www.hoddereducation.co.uk.

© Louise O'Gorman 2012
First published in 2012 by
Hodder Education,
an Hachette UK company
338 Euston Road
London NW1 3BH

Impression number   10 9 8 7 6 5 4 3 2 1
Year   2016 2015 2014 2013 2012

Cover photo © The Gallery Collection/Corbis

Typeset in Frutiger LT Std by Datapage (India) Pvt. Ltd.

Artwork by Barking Dog Art

Printed and bound in India

A catalogue record for this title is available from the British Library

ISBN 978 1 444 15854 0

Get the most from this book

This book will help you revise for the Development Study (Medicine Through Time) and the Depth Study (either The American West 1840–1895 or Germany 1919–1945) for the OCR (A) GCSE Schools History Project specification. You can use the revision planner on page 4 to plan your revision, topic by topic. Tick each box when you have:

1. revised and understood a topic

2. answered the exam practice questions

3. checked your answers online.

You can also keep track of your revision by ticking off each topic heading throughout the book. You may find it helpful to add your own notes as you work through each topic.

✓ Tick to track your progress

Examiner's tip

Throughout the book there are examiner's tips that explain how you can boost your final grade.

✓ Tick to track your progress

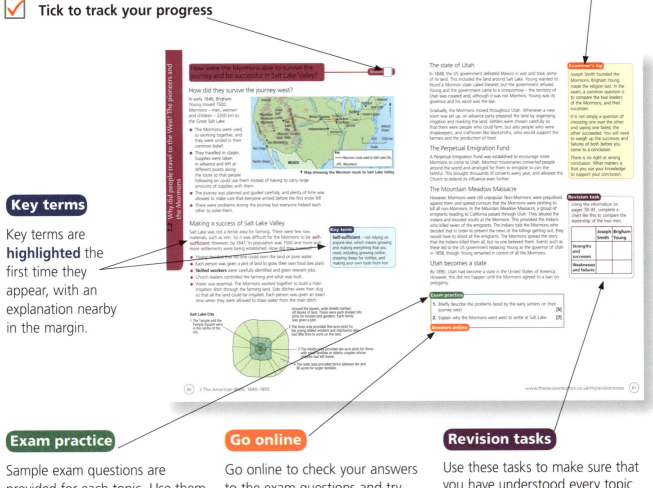

Key terms

Key terms are **highlighted** the first time they appear, with an explanation nearby in the margin.

Exam practice

Sample exam questions are provided for each topic. Use them to consolidate your revision and practise your exam skills.

Go online

Go online to check your answers to the exam questions and try out the quick quizzes at **www.therevisionbutton.co.uk/myrevisionnotes**.

Revision tasks

Use these tasks to make sure that you have understood every topic and to help you record the key information about each topic.

Contents and revision planner

Revision and exam technique

It is important that you understand that your brain is like a very, very tiny but extremely detailed, filing cabinet. When you go into an exam, the history section of it will be rammed full of content knowledge.

Revision technique gets the knowledge into the filing cabinet in the first place. **Exam technique** helps you get the right file out and ready for the examiner to read it, sorting out your knowledge into an answer that makes sense and answers the question in the exam.

Revision technique

HOW CAN I REMEMBER IT ALL ?

There are many different methods of revision and you will have your own favourites. Here are some suggestions that work particularly well for history.

Method 1: Mnemonics

Mnemonics are a really useful way of remembering linked items – chronology, several causes or aspects of a topic. You can either use the first letters of each item to make up a complete word, or you can use those letters to make up a new phrase which is easier to remember.

For example, you need to remember the chronology of the History of Medicine:

What you need to remember ...	A much easier way to remember is ...
Prehistoric **E**gyptian **G**reek **R**oman **M**iddle Ages **R**enaissance **18th**, **19th** and **20th** centuries	**P**urple **E**lephants **G**et **R**oses **M**ainly **R**ed **18**, **19** or **20** at a time!

You can make up your own mnemonics as you go through this book. Make them as silly as you want. Draw little doodles – anything that will help you to remember.

Method 2: Memory maps

Memory maps (or mind maps) are a great way to remember a whole topic like the history of medicine, or a smaller topic like why Hitler rose to power. You can:

- make links between bits of information by drawing branches or arrows
- add your own colours, doodles and mnemonics to help your memory.

It would be a really great idea for you to build up these memory maps as you revise, and then stick them up all over your home in the weeks coming up to an exam. Put one on your bedroom wall by your bed, put one next to where you eat breakfast in the morning, you could even put one on the wall next to the toilet!

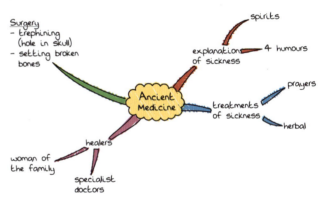

Method 3: Timelines

Timelines are always useful for history, but for the history of medicine they are **vital** because the course covers such a vast period – see pages 10–11 for some ideas from the history of medicine.

- You could create your own version of these on several pieces of paper, and put them up in the place where you are revising.
- Add colour and doodles to help you to remember things.

Method 4: Key individual profiles

For the Medicine Development Study, you need to remember and often compare the achievements of key individuals in medicine, for example: Hippocrates, Galen, Vesalius, Pasteur and others. It will help you to remember and use this information if you use the same format for each individual. A fun idea for this is to think of it as a personal profile for a social network site. This allows you to recall the important information. You can find a template like this at www.therevisionbutton.co.uk/myrevisionnotes.

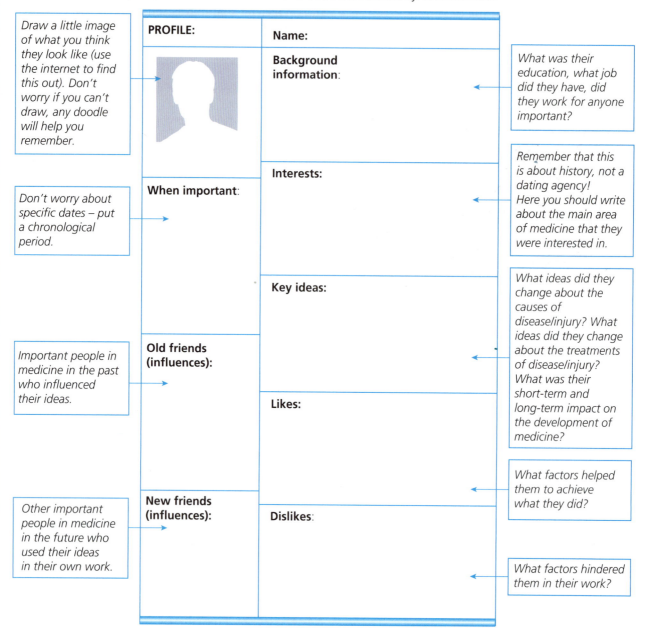

Draw a little image of what you think they look like (use the internet to find this out). Don't worry if you can't draw, any doodle will help you remember.

PROFILE:

Name:

Background information:

What was their education, what job did they have, did they work for anyone important?

Don't worry about specific dates – put a chronological period.

When important:

Interests:

Remember that this is about history, not a dating agency! Here you should write about the main area of medicine that they were interested in.

Key ideas:

What ideas did they change about the causes of disease/injury? What ideas did they change about the treatments of disease/injury? What was their short-term and long-term impact on the development of medicine?

Important people in medicine in the past who influenced their ideas.

Old friends (influences):

Likes:

What factors helped them to achieve what they did?

Other important people in medicine in the future who used their ideas in their own work.

New friends (influences):

Dislikes:

What factors hindered them in their work?

Revision tasks

Throughout the book there are **Revision tasks**.

Don't miss them out (unless you have a better way). They get you using the information rather than just reading it. The more you use it, the better you will remember it.

Other revision methods

- You could make your own 'key points' **revision cards** to carry round with you to revise on the go (see page 109).

- You could make a **recording of the text** and play it back to yourself.

- You could go online to www.therevisionbutton. co.uk/myrevisionnotes and have a go at the **quick quizzes**.

- You could **create your own tests** using the content and test your friends.

Exam technique

You will sit **two** exams during your course. They are called: A951 and A952.

Unit A951: Study in Development and Study in Depth

A951 contains your **Development Study** and **Depth Study**. It is 2 hours long. The paper has two sections:
Section A: Development Study – this book covers **Medicine Through Time** (pages 10–69)
Section B: Depth Study – this book covers **The American West, 1840–1895** (pages 70–100) and **Germany, c.1919–1945** (pages 101–128). You have to do only one of these depth studies.

Section A: Development Study:

In **Section A**, you **must** answer Question 1 then you can **choose** to answer Question 2, 3 **or** 4. You should spend about one hour on this section.

Question 1 is compulsory – you have to do it. It is based on a group of sources, often based around themes, turning points or factors. It is split into three parts, with a total of 15 marks. Spend about 25 minutes on this question.

Questions 2, 3 and 4 are based on your own knowledge of the course content. You have to answer only one of them. Each question is split into three parts, worth a total of 20 marks. Spend about 35–40 minutes on this question.

Section B: Depth study

The second section of A951 is about the depth study. You must answer Question 5, which is very similar to Question 1 of the development study, and then choose to answer either Question 6 or Question 7, which are very similar to Questions 2, 3 and 4 of the development study.

There are **common question types** that come up again and again. This page helps you to spot these questions, plan your answers and shows you what kind of answers the examiner is looking for.

Exam practice Throughout the book you can practise each question type many times. There are model answers online for you to learn from.

The **Examiner's tip** will help you further.

Part (a), the 'describe' question: This question is worth 5 marks.

It might ask you to describe the work of an individual, the impact of a particular factor, or how people in a particular period tried to prevent disease. For example:

> Briefly describe the work of Hippocrates. [5]

Example 1

Hippocrates was a famous doctor in Ancient Greece. He looked for natural explanations of disease. He came up with the Theory of the Four Humours to explain disease, which people believed for over a thousand years. He also developed the process of clinical observation. Hippocrates wrote down his ideas and his books became known as the Hippocratic collection. Another aspect of Hippocrates' work was the Hippocratic Oath. The doctor took an oath to promise to do all he could to help his patients.

Example 2

Hippocrates was a famous doctor in Ancient Greece. He looked for natural explanations of disease. He came up with the Theory of the Four Humours to explain disease. His theory was that the body contained four liquids: blood, yellow bile, black bile and phlegm which had to be in balance. People got ill when the humours were out of balance so the work of a doctor was to get the humours back in balance by bleeding (if they had too much blood) or purging (if they had too much bile).

He also developed the process of clinical observation, which meant a doctor carefully observing a patient's symptoms and writing down what he saw. The doctor should also wrote down his treatments and observe the results. In this way Hippocrates said that doctors could get better at treating illness because they would learn from past mistakes or successes.

Part (b), the 'explain' question: This question is worth 7 marks. It could ask you to explain why an individual is important in the history of medicine, or how and why something has happened. To answer this question you will need to describe then explain, using specific information to support your arguments. Here is an example.

> **Explain ways in which religion had an impact on the development of medicine during the Middle Ages.** [7]

Religion both helped and hindered the development of medicine in the Middle Ages.

One way religion hindered progress was that the Christian Church taught that illness was a punishment for sins and so during the Black Death people thought that a good treatment was to pray or to whip yourself to show God you were sorry. This belief affected the development of medicine by preventing people looking for natural explanations so treatments did not improve.

A second way was the Christian Church's support for Galen. The Church did not want anyone to argue with Galen because his ideas fitted in with Christian beliefs about the body being perfectly made. The Christian Church controlled the universities so the only sort of training that doctors were allowed at university in the early Middle Ages was to read the books of Galen – even when he was wrong. Students did not research or do dissections to find out things for themselves.

However, religion sometimes helped medicine too. For example, Jesus taught that Christians should look after the sick so Christian monks and nuns set up hospitals where sick people could be looked after, fed and kept clean or be given herbal remedies, as well as being prayed for of course!

Examiner's tip

This is a factor question. If you have been compiling a factor chart during your course you should have plenty of examples to draw on. To prepare for this question write down at least three examples of this factor (religion) either helping or hindering the development of medicine. For example:

1 the belief that illness was a punishment from God

2 Christian support for the ideas of Galen

3 Church said that Christians had a duty to look after the sick.

Make sure you have something on both sides. And the question is about religion not Christianity so you could also bring in examples from Islamic medicine.

In your answer you will need to describe each example (to show you understand it) but also explain the specific impact that this belief/idea had on medical progress. And remember once again this needs to use well-written paragraphs linking your ideas together and not be simply a list.

Part (c), the evaluation question, will ask you to evaluate a statement and explain how far you agree or disagree with it. You can't simply say you agree or disagree with the statement, you need to write a balanced answer showing that you understand both sides of the argument so that takes some planning. Use a grid like this:

The statement:	
The argument for:	The argument against:
Your conclusion:	

'The main reason why public health was improved in the 19th century was because the working classes got the vote.' How for do you agree with this statement? Explain your answer. [8]

Examiner's tip

Your answer needs to use well-written paragraphs linking your points and your evidence together. Structure your answer like this:

Paragraph 1: Introduction showing that you understand the statement.

Paragraph 2: Reasons to support the statement

Paragraph 3: Reasons to challenge it

(these two paragraphs could be the other way round)

Paragraph 4: Your conclusion. Don't sit on the fence and write a neutral answer. There is no right or wrong answer. Just make sure that what you say refers back to and builds on the points you made in paragraphs 2 and 3.

Example of using the planning grid

The statement:

'The main reason why public health was improved in the 19th century was because the working classes got the vote.'

The argument for:	The argument against:
How working classes getting the vote helped improved public health	What <u>other factors</u> helped lead to improvements in public health
● Poor were the most affected by disease and bad conditions in cities but government did not force the towns to take action they left it up to individuals to sort out the problem – laissez-faire.	● There had been lots of improvements before the working classes got the vote.
● Working classes got the vote in 1867. Politicians now realised they had to keep these new voters happy.	● Ever since Chadwick in the 1830s the government had been very worried about the living conditions of the poor.
● Public Health Act of 1875 made cleaning up towns compulsory – and the towns had to pay for it,	● Snow had worked to prevent cholera spreading in working-class London in the 1850s before working men got the vote.
● So...working class votes made the difference.	● The Great Stink was what convinced many MPs to do something to clean up the Thames.
	● And most important the link between dirt and disease had been proved scientifically following Pasteur's germ theory.

Your conclusion:

● Having considered the evidence do you agree or disagree with the statement?

● How strongly do you feel about it?

I don't really agree with the statement. Working classes getting the vote was an important factor but it was not the only one – not even the most important one. It affected the timing of the Public Health Act but other factors had paved the way.

Read the question!

One of the most common mistakes candidates make in exams is not to answer the question. And a common reason for that is that they have not read it properly! They have revised so much that when they see any particular word in a question they launch into writing everything they know about that and forget that the question has a particular focus. So one of the biggest steps you can take to improve your grade is to read the question carefully and focus your answer on what it is actually asking rather than what you would like it to be asking! It doesn't matter how much you know if you don't use it to answer the question.

For each question in the exam read it carefully to spot:

a) the question type
   (e.g. is this a 'describe' question or a 'why' question?)

b) the content focus

c) the dates or the period
   (not all questions have dates but if they do they are important)

d) number of marks
   (this helps guide you on how much to write in your answer)

Here are three examples from the three sections of this book.

1. Explain ways in which religion had an impact on the development of medicine during the Middle Ages. **[7]**

2. Describe the problems faced by the early settlers on their journey west. **[5]**

3. Why was Hitler able to increase his power between January 1933 and August 1934? **[7]**

Unit A952: Historical Source Investigation

A952 asks you to study sources about specific British case studies from the history of medicine. But you can't bluff your way through this paper without knowledge. You need to have enough background knowledge to understand the sources you are given. So remember, for this exam, source-handling skills + knowledge = success.

Each year the exam is based around a different case study. Your teacher will know what the case study is before the examination is set. Each case study is highlighted like this in the book: **Case study**

There are six compulsory questions on this paper. The examiner tips with each case study show you how to answer these question-types that could appear. So, whatever your case study is, make sure you look at the exam practice and examiner's tips for the other case studies so you are prepared for all types of questions.

The depth study examination also starts with some compulsory source-based questions. These questions ask you to use your background knowledge to understand and evaluate sources. Many question types are similar to those in the source investigation or the development study so the exam practice and tips in Section 1 will be useful there too.

Question type	Key skill	Case study	Examiner's tips
What does this source tell you about…?	Comprehension and inference	The Black Death in England	Page 34
Does this source prove that…?	Evaluation	Public Health in the Middle Ages	Page 38
How useful is this source for…?	Evaluation	Quack doctors	Page 46
How similar (or different) are…?	Cross-reference	Jenner and the vaccination debate	Page 48
		The development of hospitals	Page 56
Are you surprised by…?	Contextual understanding	The development of penicillin	Page 54
Why was Source X published in…?	Contextual understanding	Developments in anaesthetics and antiseptics	Page 60
		Public Health in the nineteenth century	Page 65

Top tips for the Source Investigation Paper

1. Read through all the **background information**, all the **sources** and all the **questions** before you start writing anything. That way you will get an overall feel for the topic and all your answers will be more informed. They will also trigger you to remember your background knowledge as well.

2. Make sure you read the **caption** to each source. This will contain important information about who wrote or created a source.

3. In your answers always say **which source you are referring to** – Source A, Source B, etc.

4. Always **support your answer with details from the sources**. Use actual words or phrases from written sources. Describe features of visual sources.

5. **Cross-reference** to other sources. Some questions will specifically ask you to do this but even when they don't it is likely that the other sources can help you. Examiners say that candidates find cross-referencing the hardest thing of all so if you do it well the examiners will be really impressed.

6. **Use your background knowledge whenever it is useful**. Background knowledge can help you to judge whether a source is reliable, or help you to know why a source was published at a particular time. However, don't include background knowledge for its own sake – only if it helps you to answer the question.

7. **Don't speculate**. Phrases like 'the author might be...' won't impress the examiner. If you know something about the author say it. If you don't then speculation won't earn you any marks.

Question 6

At the end of the Historical Source Investigation paper is the great and wonderful **Question 6**, which is worth a whopping 10 marks! Obviously there is a technique to answering this question.

The question will set a hypothesis and ask you to judge how far the sources support this hypothesis, for example:

> **'Quack doctors made little contribution to caring for the sick in the eighteenth and nineteenth centuries.' How far do the sources on this paper agree with this view? Use the sources and your knowledge to explain your answer.** [10]

You will have already looked at six or seven sources in Questions 1 to 5 and you will be asked to use them again for this question. For each source, think about the following questions:

1. Does the source support or challenge the statement?
2. Why does it agree or disagree with the statement? (It could do both.) Give an example.
3. Do you trust the source? You may have already answered a question about its reliability.

Then:

- Write one paragraph about the sources that support the statement.
- Write one paragraph about the sources that challenge the statement.
- Reach a conclusion. How far do the sources and your own knowledge support or challenge the statement?

Remember to consider the reliability of the sources. You will look a bit silly if you have said that Source B was 'completely unreliable' but then you use it to back up your hypothesis.

1 Medicine Through Time

1.1 Overview 1: Create your own thematic timeline

The history of medicine over thousands of years is a vast topic. So, to help you to focus, the course has five 'themes' or 'key questions' that are asked about each period.

- **Causes of disease**: What caused people to be healthy or unhealthy?
- **Healers**: Who provided medical care?
- **Ideas**: What ideas did people have about the causes and treatments of illness and injuries?
- **Factors**: What caused diagnoses and treatments to remain the same or to change?
- **Impact**: How far did new ideas and treatments affect the majority of the population?

<table>
<tr><td colspan="2"></td><td>Prehistoric</td><td>Egypt</td><td>Greece</td></tr>
<tr><td colspan="2">Approximate dates</td><td>3000 BC to 500 BC</td><td>2000 BC to 200 BC</td><td>1000 BC to 0 BC</td></tr>
<tr><td colspan="2">Key Question</td><td></td><td></td><td></td></tr>
<tr><td colspan="2">What caused people to be healthy or unhealthy?</td><td></td><td></td><td></td></tr>
<tr><td rowspan="2">Who provided medical care?</td><td>Natural</td><td>Women in the home</td><td>Women in the home</td><td>Women in the home</td></tr>
<tr><td>Supernatural</td><td></td><td></td><td></td></tr>
<tr><td rowspan="4">What ideas did people have about the causes and treatments of illnesses and injuries?</td><td>Natural explanations</td><td>Obvious common sense</td><td></td><td></td></tr>
<tr><td>Supernatural explanations</td><td></td><td></td><td></td></tr>
<tr><td>Natural treatments</td><td></td><td></td><td></td></tr>
<tr><td>Supernatural treatments</td><td></td><td></td><td></td></tr>
<tr><td colspan="2">Which factors caused diagnoses and treatments to remain the same or to change?</td><td></td><td></td><td>Hippocrates</td></tr>
<tr><td colspan="2">How far did new ideas and treatments affect the majority of the population?</td><td></td><td></td><td></td></tr>
</table>

Below is a template for you to create your own history of medicine overview timeline.

- Make yours as big as possible.
- As you revise the history of medicine, on pages 14–69, you will find a 'key questions table' **KQ** at the end of each topic. Each table summarises each theme for that period or topic.
- Make sure you read and revise these 'key questions tables' in order to add the information to your own overview timeline.
- You could add your own illustrations, arrows and colours to help you organise the detail.
- Making your timeline will help you to think in the way the examiner wants you to think – seeing the big picture of how and why medicine changes or stays the same across periods of history.
- Knowing how and why changes happened in each theme is the key to getting the highest grades.

Rome	Middle Ages	Renaissance	1800s, 1900s and after
450 BC to AD 753	AD 500 to AD 1500	AD 1500 to AD 1750	AD 1800 to present
	The Black Death		
Women in the home			
The gods	Sent by God as punishment		
			So much happened in this period that you will need lots of space. See detailed timeline on page 50.
Public health for all			
Rich people did better			

1.2 Overview 2: Turning points and factors

Turning points in the history of medicine

There are times in history when understanding of disease or treatment changes dramatically and decisively. These are **turning points**.

Revision task

You must know what the turning points are. The examiners will expect you to identify them without being prompted. But don't panic – here is a list of turning points that you must really know about! Make a revision card for each turning point. On one side, write the turning point and the date, and on the other side summarise:

- who was involved
- what happened
- what changed as a result in the short term and the long term.

Turning point	Date	Page	Summary
1 Hippocrates develops: **a** the theory of the four humours	5th/4th century BC	23	Ideas about natural causes of disease are now as important and common as supernatural (rather than just common sense ideas).
b clinical observation	5th/4th century BC	24	Doctors have rules to follow and spread their methods.
2 Vesalius makes detailed anatomical drawings	1530s–1560s	42	He proved Galen wrong and challenged Greek and Roman ideas by dissection of humans.
3 Paré tries out new surgical methods	1530s–1560s	43	New methods of surgery, written down in books so that the ideas spread. Ideas do not work very effectively until the development of antiseptics.
4 Harvey studies the heart	1620s–1650s	43	Challenge made to Greek and Roman ideas; proved by experiments.
5 Smallpox vaccination	1790s	48	Prevention of the infectious disease smallpox. Leads to vaccinations against other diseases.
6 Pasteur develops germ theory	1860s	52	Once the link between germs and disease is proved and understood, developments 7–12 become possible.
7 Simpson develops anaesthetics	1840s	59	More complex operations are possible.
8 Lister develops effective antiseptics	1860s	60	Antiseptics mean that operations are now a safe way to treat illnesses and injury rather than a last resort.
9 Nightingale improves hospitals and nursing practices	1850s	57	Clean hospitals mean that people who visit hospital do not die. No longer a last resort.
10 Public Health Act 1875	1875	65	Conditions in towns are cleaner which leads to the end of disease, and later on to improvements in living conditions – housing, etc.
11 Ehrlich creates the first magic bullet	1911	53	Cure for syphilis. Leads to chemical cures for other diseases.
12 Discovery of penicillin	1928	54	A cure for infectious diseases developed most infectious diseases are now treatable with antibiotics.

Factors and how they affect the history of medicine

Many questions in your exam will ask you about 'factors'. These are things that:

- **helped to cause change** – for example, the factor of **chance** led Paré to try out a different method of treating gunshot wounds when he accidentally ran out of oil
- **helped to prevent change** – for example, the factor of **religion** hindered knowledge of anatomy in the Middle Ages as the Church banned dissection.

The main factors are shown in the table below, along with examples of how they helped or hindered change.

> **Revision task**
>
> Make your own chart or table for each period to record examples. You can download a template from www.therevisionbutton.co.uk/myrevisionnotes.

Factor	Explanation of factor	Examples of helping change	Examples of hindering change
Religion	Anything to do with gods or spirits. Organised religion becomes a real factor from the Egyptians onwards.	*In the Middle Ages it helped because there was a duty to care for the sick in Islam and Christianity. (page 33)*	
War	When countries were fighting each other.	*Pasteur and Koch were French and German. They were making their findings during the Franco (France)–Prussian (German) war. This meant that they were competing all the time, both scientifically and for their country's honour. (page 54)*	
Government	The influence of laws and other rules on people's health.		*Governments did little to improve public health in the nineteenth century because of 'laissez-faire' (page 64)*
Individual genius	An individual and their story, where they made the effort or had the expertise to change things.	*Hippocrates was a brilliant thinker who came up with the theory of the four humours and the method of clinical observation. (pages 25–26)*	
Chance	Luck, something that happens by accident!	*Fleming didn't wash up his petri dishes, and found penicillin living in them – which led to its use as a life-saving drug. (page 54)*	
Communication	This is about people communicating their ideas and sharing them so that they can build on each other's ideas.	*During the Renaissance, the printing press allowed books to be published widely and men like Paré, Vesalius and Harvey could spread their ideas quickly. (page 43)*	
Science and technology	Science is anything involving experiments or careful observation. Technology is the use of equipment.	*Science: Pasteur proved his germ theory using scientific methods. (page 52)*	
Conservatism	People prevent change because they don't want to try out something new.		*Doctors opposed the NHS because they would lose money and freedom (page 49)*

1.3 Prehistoric times

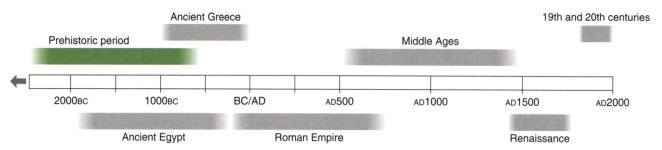

Prehistoric period · Ancient Greece · Ancient Egypt · Roman Empire · Middle Ages · Renaissance · 19th and 20th centuries

2000BC · 1000BC · BC/AD · AD500 · AD1000 · AD1500 · AD2000

Prehistoric people were **hunter-gatherers**.

- **Hunter** – they hunted animals for food.
- **Gatherer** – they collected berries, nuts and other plants for food.
- Because they were looking for animals and food, they had to travel around rather than living in the same place – they were **nomadic**. To survive, prehistoric people had to be fit and healthy – travelling across long distances was hard work, hunting for food was dangerous. Many mothers and babies died in childbirth from complications. **Life expectancy was low** (about 19–25 years).

> **Key term**
>
> **Prehistoric** – before writing began. In Britain, this means before the Romans arrived in AD 43

> **Key content**
>
> - The nature of the evidence, its values and its problems
> - Beliefs in spirits and the treatments used by medicine men
> - Practical knowledge and resulting treatments

The nature of the evidence, its values and its problems

Revised

It is very difficult to find out exactly how people lived in prehistoric times because:

- they **moved around all the time** and did not settle and build things that lasted
- they had **no written language**, so there are no written records. This means there are no descriptions about what they did to improve people's health and treat illnesses.

However, we can use the following methods to make some educated guesses about the ways of life of the people who lived in prehistoric times:

- looking at other **hunter-gatherer societies** – good examples are records of the **Plains Indians** who lived in North America in the nineteenth century, and what we know about the **Aborigines** who still exist in **Australia**
- looking at **what was written about hunter-gatherers** by the **Egyptians** and the **Romans**
- looking at **artefacts: bones, skulls** and **cave paintings** that have survived for approximately 3000 years (from prehistoric times).

> **Key term**
>
> **Aborigines** – native people of Australia who are hunter-gatherers

Beliefs in spirits and the treatments used by medicine men

Revised

People living in prehistoric times believed in **spirits**. They believed that spirits were in every natural living thing – in trees, in animals and in humans – and that they were involved in every part of their world – life, death, health and disease. **Natural and supernatural existed side by side**. Prehistoric people knew little about the real causes of disease. When they couldn't understand why people got infected and became ill, they looked to the spirit world for an explanation.

Supernatural explanations of illness

- **Evil spirits** accidentally entering a person's body.
- **People putting a curse on someone** and making an evil spirit enter their body by chanting and pointing at them with a **pointing bone**.
- **People losing their own spirits** – usually because of a curse.

Supernatural treatments of illness

A **medicine man** provided spiritual comfort and medical help. He would work out what the cause of the illness was by contacting the spirit world and then decide on a treatment:

- **By chanting** and **dancing** the medicine man would get very hot and go into a trance to contact the spirits to get rid of the evil spirits.
- **Charms** were given to people to warn off evil spirits.
- **Trephining** (also known as trepanning) – boring a hole into the skull to allow the spirit to escape the body. The hole was created by a **stone knife** (there were no metal tools at this time). Skulls have been found where the bone has grown back over the hole, which shows us that some people **survived** for months (or years) after the operation.

However, the history of medicine is never simple. In most periods, people combine natural and supernatural explanations and treatments so it is no surprise that medicine men also used natural **herbal remedies** described in the section below.

> **Examiner's tip**
>
> Make sure that you understand the difference between the **supernatural** spiritual explanations and cures used in medicine and the **natural** explanations and cures. This is one of the **big ideas** in the Medicine course. It comes up again and again through each period. You should gather examples of each in your overview chart (page 11).

Practical knowledge and resulting treatments

Revised

Natural treatments of illness

When someone was sick, prehistoric people would commonly use **natural remedies** such as herbs, plants, minerals and animal parts. The **women** of the tribe **learned remedies from their own mothers**, which came from a process of observation and **trial and error**. For example, the Plains Indians used squaw root to relax the uterus during childbirth, which helped with the pain. We know that a form of aspirin was made from the leaves of willow trees, which was used as we use it today as a painkiller and to stop inflammation. Even though they didn't know *how* this worked, they knew it *did* work and so continued to use it. If these natural remedies didn't work, they turned to the medicine men.

Natural treatments of injuries

Injuries from hunting, accidents or fighting against other tribes were treated using **common sense**. **Mud** was used to set broken limbs and **splints made of wood** were used.

Copy and complete the table below to create a revision table about treatments in prehistoric times. You may not be able to fill in all the cells.

Treatment	What sort of illnesses/injuries did this treat?	Who used the treatment?	Was this a natural/ common sense or supernatural treatment?
Chanting or dancing	*Anything that didn't get better through other methods*		
Splints/mud			
Herbal remedies			*Natural*
Trephining			

Exam practice

1. Briefly describe the methods used by people in prehistoric times to treat illness. **[5]**

Answers online

Examiner's tip

This is a 'describe' question. Use the guidance on page 7 to help you. Be sure to mention both natural and supernatural treatments.

Revision task

Add information from this table to your thematic timeline from pages 10–11.

KQ

Key question	Prehistoric medicine
What caused people to be healthy or unhealthy?	– Injuries from hunting or fighting – Childbirth complications (needed to be treated so that the tribe would survive)
Who provided medical care?	– Women with natural remedies – Medicine men if the problem did not get better – to get rid of spirits
What ideas did people have about the **causes** and **treatment** of illness and injuries?	**Causes:** *natural* – accidents from hunting or fighting *supernatural* – spirits, losing a spirit or having an evil spirit **Treatments:** *natural* – herbs, plants, minerals, animal parts, mud and splints for broken bones *supernatural* – chanting, dancing, charms, trephining
What caused diagnoses and treatments to remain the same or to change?	Remained the same because 'lifestyle' stayed the same – people spent all their time hunting and gathering to survive rather than thinking about medicine
How far did new ideas and treatments affect the majority of the population?	Any new treatments spread slowly as communications were slow

1.4 Ancient Egypt

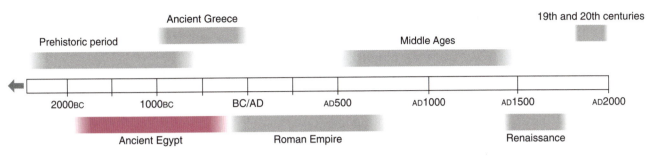

2000BC	1000BC	BC/AD	AD500	AD1000	AD1500	AD2000

Prehistoric period

Ancient Greece

Middle Ages

19th and 20th centuries

Ancient Egypt

Roman Empire

Renaissance

A big change in civilisation came when **hunter-gatherers began to settle in one place** as they realised that they could grow crops or keep their own animals for food. The first places where this happened were along the great rivers of the world where the soil was more fertile. One of these places was in Egypt along the **River Nile**.

Key content

- The development of Egyptian civilisation and its impact on medicine
- The co-existence in Egyptian society of spiritual and natural beliefs and treatments
- Developments in the understanding of physiology, anatomy and the causes of disease
- Egyptian hygiene

The development of Egyptian civilisation and its impact on medicine

Revised ☐

There were **seven** important developments in Egyptian civilisation that had an impact on the development of medicine:

1 FARMING Egyptian civilisation developed along the **River Nile**. The Nile floods annually, which keeps the surrounding area fertile. Farmers could channel the water from the Nile to their fields so their crops got plenty of water (**irrigation**). Farming was so successful that Egypt became very wealthy. Rich people had time and money to spend on other things such as medicine or religion.

2 The people who had contact with the spirit world were now called **priests** rather than medicine men. They organised the belief in the spirit world into a **RELIGION**. With this came the ideas of **the afterlife**, and that the spirits were now **gods** that were in control of different aspects of the world.

↑ Egypt and the River Nile

3 WRITTEN LANGUAGE also developed through using signs called hieroglyphics. This allowed **ideas and thoughts to be written down and shared**. Historians have been able to read these documents – this is why we know a lot more about Egyptian medicine than prehistoric medicine.

4 More complicated TOOLS were developed, which could be used for medicine.

5 The role of DOCTORS became more important. They were carefully trained, and the idea of going to a doctor for help became more common than in prehistoric times. Doctors were still religious figures and used charms, prayers and chants as well as natural remedies.

6 As people settled in one place, **CITIES** developed. **Cities caused some problems** for the people who lived there. The first was how to get rid of their **waste**. This was solved by the River Nile in Egypt! The second was **epidemics** which spread quickly where many people were settled.

7 TRADE was developed – goods were traded with other countries. This included medical herbs and other natural remedies. **Medical ideas were also spread** this way.

> **Revision task**
>
> Think of your own mnemonic (see page 5) to help you to remember these seven developments that affected medicine in Egypt: **f**arming, **r**eligion, **w**riting, **t**ools, **d**octors, **c**ities, **t**rade.

The co-existence in Egyptian society of spiritual and natural beliefs and treatments

Revised

The Egyptians believed that the gods controlled everything in life, including the flooding of the Nile and when people got sick. However, just as in prehistoric times, **natural and supernatural ideas existed side by side**.

Basic treatment started in the home with herbal remedies, but if you were rich enough or a condition was serious enough, you would be treated at a **temple**. Priests would use **common sense treatments** alongside **supernatural treatments**. They did not make the distinction between them that we make today. Specialist **doctors**, or **physicians** who were also priests, were employed by the pharaohs and often had other skills apart from medicine. For example, **Imhotep**, the Pharaoh's doctor, was also an architect, a chief minister and in later inscriptions was called a god on earth! Another doctor was the famous 'guardian of the anus', **Irj**.

> **Examiner's tip**
>
> Egyptian medicine is a good example of the factor of communication at work. **Communication** is about the **recording** and **sharing** of ideas and is *just* as important in the history of medicine as any of the methods used to cure people. If someone finds a new treatment, it only affects others if they communicate it!
>
> This begins in Ancient Egypt through writing. People wrote things down using **hieroglyphics**, so ideas about how to treat people were spread much further and more quickly than they could be from one person to another by word of mouth. **Trade** between countries spread the ideas more widely.

> **Examiner's tip**
>
> If you remember only one thing about Egyptian medicine, remember 'specialist doctors'. They were a cross between priests and doctors but became quite specialised in treating particular parts of the body.

> **Key term**
>
> **Physician** – another name for a doctor

Natural beliefs and treatments

Disease – they looked to nature and the world around them for some explanations of illness and disease, for example, 'blocked channels' (see page 20).

Injuries – they had a good understanding of injuries that could happen at work, during battles and when hunting animals. When injuries had an obvious cause, like a broken bone from falling or a bite from an animal, they used natural treatments.

Treatments – they made natural treatments from **herbs**, **plants**, **minerals** and **animal parts** to treat injury and everyday illness. For example, Egyptians used **honey**, a natural antiseptic, to treat many conditions (see Source A).

Supernatural beliefs and treatments

For injuries and disease that didn't have obvious causes, for example internal injuries, the Egyptians believed that they **were sent by the gods and could be cured by them**. For example, **Sekhmet** was the bringer of epidemics and **Bes** looked after women in childbirth. Some doctors became gods after they died, such as the Pharaoh's doctor **Imhotep**.

Treatment – spells, charms and **prayers** were used.

The Egyptians knew about many parts of the human body. They didn't learn about the body by medical **dissection** because their religion said **the body was needed in the after-life**. They believed that as the sun set on the land of the living, it rose in the land of the dead. When people died, they believed they would move to the land of the dead, so they would need their bodies.

So how did they look inside bodies, and why? The bodies that were buried in pyramids or hidden tombs would rot very quickly unless they were **preserved** in some way – so priests made them into **mummies** through the process of **embalming**. The dead bodies were opened up and herbs were put inside to preserve them. Vital organs (stomach, intestines, lungs and liver) were taken out and put in four separate canopic jars. Using a hook, the brain was taken out of the body through the nose. Through this process Egyptian doctors/ priests found out about the inside of the human body.

> **Key terms**
>
> **Dissection** – the careful cutting and analysis of dead bodies
>
> **Embalming** – preserving the body for burial

> **Source A:** *From Ebers Papyrus c.1500 BC*
>
> 'For the evacuation of the belly: Cow's milk, 1; grains, 1; honey 1; mash, sift, cook; take in four portions.'

> **Examiner's tip**
>
> Candidates ask, 'How much do I need to know?' Good question, and it varies from topic to topic, but a helpful rule is always to have two examples to support any point you want to make. For example:
>
> - 2 Egyptian gods
> - 2 Egyptian doctors
> - 2 Egyptian treatments.

> **Revision task**
>
> Read Source B. Label the stick figure below to show which parts of a person Irj would treat.
>
>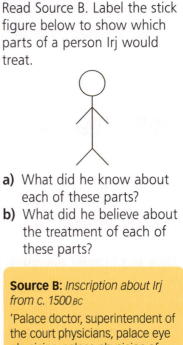
>
> a) What did he know about each of these parts?
> b) What did he believe about the treatment of each of these parts?

> **Source B:** *Inscription about Irj from c. 1500 BC*
>
> 'Palace doctor, superintendent of the court physicians, palace eye physician, palace physician of the belly and one who understands the internal fluids and who is guardian of the anus.'

Developments in the understanding of physiology, anatomy and the causes of disease

Revised ☐

Blocked channels: a natural explanation of disease

Egyptians believed in supernatural explanations for illness and disease, but they also looked to the world around them for natural explanations.

They knew that the body contained veins and arteries that carried blood around the body. They compared these with the River Nile and the channels that they used for irrigating their crops. If the irrigation channels were blocked, water would not get through and their crops would die. In the same way, they believed that a cause of illness was when veins and arteries in the human body were **blocked**.

Treatments for illnesses therefore involved preventing these blockages, such as making the patient **bleed, vomit or empty their bowels** (**purging**).

Key term

Purging – vomiting or emptying the bowels

Revision task

Copy and complete the diagram below to make notes about the main explanations and treatments used in Egyptian medicine. You could add your own diagrams to help you to remember.

Natural explanations of illness	Supernatural explanations of illness
Natural treatments of illness	Supernatural treatments of illness

Egyptian hygiene

Revised ☐

The Egyptians took great care of their bodies:

- **They used baths** – they washed twice a day and kept clean, especially when worshipping.
- **They used toilets** – a seat with a hole cut in it with a cup or bowl underneath.
- **They slept under mosquito nets.**

The Egyptians did these things for **their own comfort and beliefs**, not because they knew what caused diseases. For example:

- They used mosquito nets to prevent bites which were uncomfortable, rather than to prevent malaria.
- They washed to please the gods when worshipping and so kept clean.
- They also wore eye make-up to make them look beautiful, but they probably didn't know that the elements it contained, such as copper ore or malachite, prevented eye infections.

Key term

Hygiene – keeping clean, from the Greek name for Asclepius' daughter Hygeia

Revision task

How did the factors below affect Egyptian medicine? Add examples to your factor chart (see page 13) using your knowledge and the notes in this topic.

RELIGION: hint – keeping clean, embalming
COMMUNICATION: hint – trade with other countries, sharing ideas

Examiner's tip

- Questions 1 and 2 are 'describe' questions. Use the guidance on pages 5–6 to help you to answer these questions.

- Remember to write in paragraphs. Don't just make a list.

- Make sure you read the questions carefully – question 2 is about staying healthy, not curing illness!

- Question 3 is an 'explain' question. Use the guidance on page 8 to help you to answer this question. Focus on two factors – you could use religion (embalming) and communication (writing). Don't just describe the factor, explain, with examples, how it helped to improve medical knowledge.

KQ

Key question	Egyptian medicine
What caused people to be healthy or unhealthy?	– Epidemics could spread in cities more than among hunter-gatherers – Washing for the gods kept people healthy
Who provided medical care?	– Women at home, using natural remedies – Doctors – usually connected to temple
What ideas did people have about the **causes** and **treatment** of illness and injuries?	**Causes:** *natural* – blockage of the veins and arteries *supernatural* – the gods, for example Sekhmet who sent epidemics **Treatments:** *natural* – bleeding, purging, natural remedies *supernatural* – praying to the gods
What caused diagnoses and treatments to remain the same or to change?	– Writing – they could keep records and share information – Religion – embalming, which led to better knowledge of the body – Compared veins to irrigation channels
How far did new ideas and treatments affect the majority of the population?	Embalming and medical treatment was for the very rich

1.5 Ancient Greece

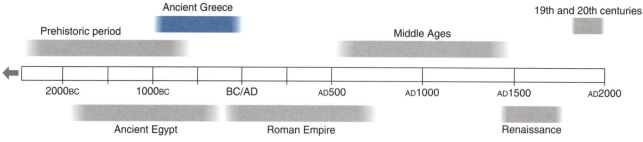

Prehistoric period

Ancient Greece

19th and 20th centuries

Middle Ages

| 2000BC | 1000BC | BC/AD | AD500 | AD1000 | AD1500 | AD2000 |

Ancient Egypt

Roman Empire

Renaissance

Ancient Greek civilisation began in about 1000 BC and the Greek Empire extended to Italy, Sicily and North Africa. It lasted until the Romans took control from around 250 BC. The Greek army, which was very effective, took over countries and areas quickly and made sure that there was peace in these places.

Some Greek people became rich from trading goods, and this meant they could **spend their time thinking and learning** instead of working in the fields. **Hippocrates** was one of these great thinkers and he investigated medicine and changed the way people thought about it.

The Greeks believed in many **different gods** who were led from Mount Olympus by Zeus. There were gods for every different aspect of life, for example a god of war, a god of wisdom and a god of wine. These beliefs were not separated from ordinary life, but part of it. For example, if there was a good harvest it meant that the gods were pleased, but if there was an earthquake it meant that the gods were angry. **Natural and supernatural ideas existed side by side in their world.**

Key content

- Asclepius and temple medicine
- The theory of the four humours and resulting treatments
- Health and hygiene
- Hippocrates and the clinical method of observation
- Developments in knowledge of anatomy and surgery at Alexandria

Asclepius and temple medicine

Revised

- **Asclepius** was the **Greek god of medicine**. The Greeks believed that he could cure most illnesses.
- Cures by Asclepius took place at an **Asclepion** (see plan on the right).
- Cures involved natural methods including **bathing, exercising and sleep** as well as using **natural remedies**. Look at the buildings on the plan to see where this happened.
- Patients believed that, while they were asleep, **Asclepius and his daughters would visit them** and complete the cures.

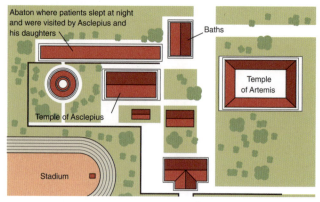

↑ **Plan of an Asclepion**

The theory of the four humours and resulting treatments

Revised

The Greeks were very interested in nature and how it affected them. They developed a theory (based on what they saw around them every day), that the world was made of **four elements**, water, earth, fire and air, and that these linked to the **four seasons** of the year.

From this, **Hippocrates**, a doctor and great thinker, developed his **theory of the four humours**. He thought that everybody was made up **of four humours** which **had to be in balance** if a person was to be healthy.

The four humours were:

BLOOD	PHLEGM	YELLOW BILE	BLACK BILE

If a person was sick, he believed that the person had too much or too little of one humour.

The theory of the four humours affected diagnosis and treatment for over 1500 years.

Link to the seasons: Greeks watched their patients very carefully. They saw that at certain times of the year certain symptoms were more common than others and they linked the four humours to the four seasons of the year. In the spring, fever was common – patients were hot and moist because of their temperature. The Greeks believed this was because they had too much blood.

Treatments involved balancing the humours. This could be done by bleeding a patient who had too much blood, or advising exercise for patients who had too little bile.

Key term

Theory of the four humours – doctors from the time of the Ancient Greeks until the Renaissance believed the four humours – blood, phlegm, yellow bile and black bile – needed to be balanced to ensure good health

Health and hygiene

Revised

The Greeks wanted to keep healthy.

- At an Asclepion, Greek patients would **exercise**, **bathe** and **sleep**.
- Hippocrates and his followers would suggest personalised health regimes for different people.
- Rich people would be advised to **rest and relax** as they could afford to do so.
- Poorer patients needed to be **given medicines** as they could not stop working to rest and relax.

As always, women provided the bulk of the care for people who were ill, usually at home. Childbirth was still very dangerous and women needed midwives to support them when they were giving birth.

Hippocrates and the clinical method of observation

Hippocrates wrote down his methods in books. These became known as the **Hippocratic Collection**. He emphasised that doctors should use clinical observation to watch and record symptoms and cures.

Clinical observation allowed doctors to build up a collection of notes with information about different symptoms, which treatments they tried and whether they worked. This helped with the diagnoses and treatment of future patients. Doctors today use clinical observation when they keep notes on you. Early doctors did exactly the same.

↑ **Examples of books in the Hippocratic Collection**

Clinical observation and treatment involves trust between the doctor and patient. Hippocrates and his followers swore a **Hippocratic Oath** in which they promised to do their patient no harm and to keep the conversation between patient and doctor confidential. **Doctors still take this oath today**.

> **Key term**
>
> **Clinical observation** – observing symptoms at a patient's bedside

> **Key term**
>
> **Hippocratic Oath** – the oath taken by doctors

> **Revision task**
>
> One way to help you to revise the key individuals such as Hippocrates is to imagine what they might put on a social networking profile. Make a profile for Hippocrates. Use the plan on page 4.

> **Revision task**
>
> Here is a visual (and silly) way to help you to remember the key things about Hippocrates.
>
> - Hippocrates
> - Ancient Greece
> - The four humours
> - Clinical observation
>
> Think about a hippo sitting on a crate full of bottles of grease (Hippocrates from Greece). He's wearing glasses (observation). On each of his four knees he has drawn a laughing face (the four humours – laughing, humour, get it?).

Developments in knowledge of anatomy and surgery at Alexandria

Revised ☐

Alexander the Great was one of the most famous people in Greek civilisation. He conquered Egypt around 330 BC and built a city called Alexandria. In this city, he built a great library which contained medical books from around the world, including the books on medicine by Hippocrates.

Unlike the rest of the Greek Empire, dissection was allowed at Alexandria. This led to doctors having more knowledge about anatomy and surgery.

Revision task

Create your factor chart for Ancient Greece (see pages 12–13) using your knowledge and the notes in this topic. You should find good examples of religion and individuals.

Exam practice

1. Briefly describe the work of Hippocrates. **[5]**

2. Explain why the Greeks were able to make so much progress in medicine. **[7]**

3. Explain why the Greeks used both natural and supernatural approaches to medicine. **[7]**

Answers online

KQ

Key question	Greek medicine
What caused people to be healthy or unhealthy?	– Injuries from farming, hunting or fighting – Childbirth complications – Epidemics could spread in cities
Who provided medical care?	– Women at home with natural remedies – Doctors who followed Hippocrates' theories and used natural methods – Medical care was given in Asclepions where religion was used as well as other more natural methods
What ideas did people have about the **causes** and **treatment** of illness and injuries?	**Causes:** *natural* – imbalance of the four humours *supernatural* – gods such as Asclepius **Treatments:** *natural* – bleeding, purging, exercising, natural remedies *supernatural* – going to an Asclepion
What caused diagnoses and treatments to remain the same or to change?	Changed – Hippocrates came up with the theory of the four humours about how the body worked, and treatments based on this, as well as the practice of clinical observation
How far did new ideas and treatments affect the majority of the population?	Mainly affected richer people, but treatments based on the four humours, such as purging, did not have to be expensive and so could be used by more people

1.6 Ancient Rome

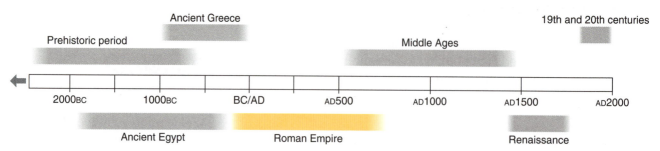

The Romans come after the Greeks in the history of medicine. The Romans were invaders. As well as invading everywhere else in Europe and in North Africa, including Egypt, they invaded Greece. They copied as many good ideas as they could from the places they invaded to use in their own civilisation. **The Romans copied ideas about medicine from the Greeks** but their own ideas were much more important.

↑ **The Roman Empire in c.120 AD**

> ## Key content
> - Comparing Roman medicine and Greek medicine
> - The Romans and public health
> - Galen's ideas about physiology, anatomy and treatment

Comparing Roman medicine and Greek medicine

 Revised

Similarities between Greek and Roman medicine

Most Roman ideas were the same as the Greeks':

- Hippocrates' ideas such as the theory of the **four humours** and **clinical observation** continued to be used.

- The Romans believed in **gods** like the Greeks and even borrowed some Greek gods. In the early days of the Roman Empire, there was a terrible plague and the Romans asked their gods for it to end. But this didn't work, so they 'borrowed' the god **Asclepius** from the Greeks and asked him to help them! From then on they built temples to Asclepius all around the Roman Empire.

- Medicine was centred round the **home** and herbal remedies were used by the women in the family who passed their ideas from mother to daughter.

Differences between Greek and Roman medicine

- The Romans believed that **'bad air'** or bad smells made people ill. To prevent bad air and bad smells, they kept themselves clean and did not build towns near marshes – which can be very pongy!

- Romans weren't as bothered about doctors as the Greeks. In fact Pliny, a Roman writer, thought that all doctors were money grabbers! Any doctors who were around in the Roman Empire were usually either Greek or trained by the Greeks. The Romans preferred not to get ill in the first place and doctors were a last resort – they believed in **prevention rather than cure**, which leads to the Romans' big idea: **public health**.

> **Revision task**
>
> Create your factor chart for Ancient Rome (see pages 12–13) using your knowledge and the notes in this topic. Make sure you record examples for religion, war, government and individual genius.

> **Key term**
>
> **Public health** – governments providing schemes to make their citizens healthier

The Romans and public health

The Romans invaded and took control of many countries which made up the Roman Empire. To invade and control countries, the Romans needed a **strong army**. They had many **army surgeons** who would treat soldiers who were injured or ill but the army also needed to be **kept healthy**.

There were many large cities in the Roman Empire and **people lived cramped together** – they knew that this could lead to unhealthy living conditions and diseases could spread quickly. The Romans wanted the people living in their Empire to be kept **healthy**. Healthy people meant more workers paying more taxes to Rome, and workers were less likely to rebel.

The Romans' big idea was public health. This was to keep their armies strong and their citizens healthy. The public health schemes that they provided were:

- **public toilets**, so waste could go into the sewers instead of onto the streets
- **public baths** for washing and exercise
- **sewers** to remove waste which emptied into rivers
- **clean water** to wash in, brought into towns from springs in the countryside via **aqueducts**
- **public fountains** and running water for drinking and washing
- **free hospitals** for soldiers.

The Romans were able to create these schemes because:

- **they were brilliant engineers and builders** and so were able to design and create the sewers and the aqueducts that were needed
- **they were very rich** as they took lots of taxes from the countries they controlled, so could pay for what was needed.

Roman public health was not all wonderful. Plagues often spread in the large cities of the Empire and when public health did not work, the Romans asked Asclepius for help. Sewers could spread disease, as could people throwing dirty water out of the windows and into the River Tiber.

↑ **Public toilets**

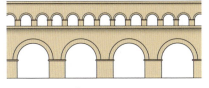

↑ **Aqueduct**

Revision task

Look at the sentence starters below, which summarise Roman ideas about public health. Complete each sentence to explain

a) what the Romans did to improve public health, and
b) why they did this. Use the words in the box in your answers.

Try to link these words together in a single answer. You will need to use some words more than once.

Sentence starters

Bad air and bad smells cause people to be unhealthy. To get rid of bad air and bad smells, the Romans built ... because ...

Prevention is better than cure. To prevent illnesses, the Romans ... because ...

Gods could cure illnesses. To ask the gods to cure them, the Romans ... because ...

It is important to keep the army healthy. To do this, the Romans ... because ...

- public baths
- public toilets
- aqueducts
- sewers
- temples to Asclepius
- hospitals and free doctors

Galen's ideas about physiology, anatomy and treatment

Revised

Claudius **Galen** was born in Greece in AD 129. He started studying medicine at the age of sixteen and became a surgeon looking after **gladiators**. This meant that he carried out simple operations and saw the insides of human bodies. If you're squeamish you may not like to think about this, but he saw inside the bodies of the gladiators because they could be cut open when they were fighting.

After this, he moved to Rome to become doctor to the Emperor – a very, very important job.

Galen wrote many books about medicine. His ideas **followed** on from those of **Hippocrates** – the theory of the four humours and clinical observation. However, he developed his own **theory of opposites** to treat people; for example, if a disease was caused by cold, his treatment was to use heat by treating the disease with hot ingredients such as peppers.

Unlike Hippocrates who didn't think dissection was important, Galen was very interested in anatomy and liked to **dissect animals** – mainly monkeys, which were most like humans, and pigs. Sometimes he was lucky enough to find a dead human that he could study. Through this he found out a lot about how the body worked.

- He had a theory about how the brain controlled the voice which he was able to prove through an experiment where he cut the nerves of a pig to stop it squealing.
- He also proved that arteries and veins carried blood around the body.
- However, he had other theories that were wrong – he thought the blood was made by the liver, and used up as fuel for the muscles. He did not realise that the same blood circulated again and again.

Galen's ideas were used for medical training for the next 1500 years. There are three reasons for this:

| 1. **His ideas fitted in with what the Christian Church believed in** – that humans were created by God and so all the parts of the body fitted together perfectly as God had planned it. In the fourth century, Christianity became the official religion of the Roman Empire. | 2. **No one could prove him wrong** – doctors didn't dissect people because it was against the law. | 3. **He wrote lots of books about his ideas** and he was so convincing that people believed that his books had all the answers. |

Examiner's tip

Don't worry too much about the differences between anatomy and physiology: they are usually used together. Anatomy is how the body is put together and physiology is how it works. With Galen, anatomy is, for example, his study of the jaw bone; physiology is, for example, the work he did about blood and the heart.

Key term

Theory of opposites – Galen's idea that you should treat a condition with its opposite

Revision task

Create a social network profile for Galen, using the guidance on page 4.

Revision task

Candidates often mix up Hippocrates and Galen. They are both important but for different things. The following statements are true for either Hippocrates or Galen or for both of them. Make a large version of the Venn diagram on the right and, using your knowledge of this topic, put the statements in the correct place.

Hippocrates / Galen

1. He developed the theory of the four humours.
2. He wrote books about medicine.
3. He was interested in anatomy.
4. He was a doctor.
5. He developed the use of opposites.
6. He was Greek.
7. The people he treated believed in Asclepius.
8. He lived in Rome.
9. His ideas were believed for at least a thousand years.
10. Some of his theories were wrong.
11. He was interested in the whole body.

Exam practice

1. Explain why Galen is important in the history of medicine. **[7]**

2. 'The Romans are more important than the Greeks in the history of medicine.' How far do you agree with this statement? Explain your answer. **[8]**

Answers online

Examiner's tip

There is a lot you could say for Question 1 so you need to focus. Concentrate on what Galen said about anatomy – the way that the body worked – and how this affected people later in history.

Examiner's tip

Question 2 is a common type of question to compare two periods. There is no right answer, but you need to include:

● what each civilisation did that was unique
● what the Romans borrowed from the Greeks
● your judgement based on the above.

Revision task

On page 24 there was a silly mnemonic about Hippocrates. Here is another silly one to help you to remember the key facts about Galen.

Think about **G**alen **r**iding **o**n **a** **d**onkey:

Galen **R**ome **O**pposites **A**natomy **D**issection

Draw your own picture!

KQ

Key question	Roman medicine
What caused people to be healthy or unhealthy?	– Injuries in battles – Problem of hygiene which developed in big cities, especially Rome
Who provided medical care?	– Family provided medical care first – Prevention rather than cure so public health was important and provided by the Romans – Doctors were a final resort – Priests at Asclepions were used if the person was rich and desperate – Army surgeons
What ideas did people have about the **causes** and **treatment** of illness and injuries?	**Causes:** *natural* – imbalance of four humours, bad air and smells *supernatural* – gods such as Asclepius **Treatments:** *natural* – use of four humours (bleeding, purging), public health schemes, opposites, herbal remedies *supernatural* – praying to Asclepius for a cure
What caused diagnoses and treatments to remain the same or to change?	Galen's use of opposites was an extension of the four humours rather than a new theory altogether
How far did new ideas and treatments affect the majority of the population?	– Little changed for people in the countryside – Most people in cities were affected by public health – baths and toilets were cheap – Rich people could afford doctors and Asclepions

1.7 The Middle Ages (1): The impact of war and religion

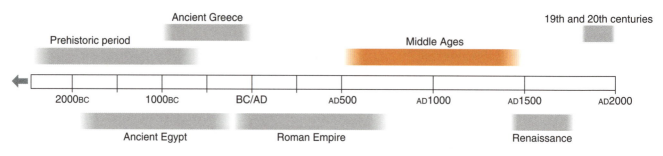

The Middle Ages lasted a long time, but very little happened in medicine! The collapse of the Roman Empire and the wars that followed had an impact at the start of the Middle Ages, but there were very few improvements in medicine for a thousand years because of one main reason: **the influence of the Church** and religion.

Key content

- The impact of the collapse of the Roman Empire on medicine
- The impact of Christianity and Islam on medicine
- The reasons for the acceptance of Galenic medicine
- The continuation of supernatural beliefs and treatments
- Case study: The Black Death in England

The impact of the collapse of the Roman Empire on medicine

Revised ☐

For hundreds of years, the Roman Empire dominated Europe and North Africa. All the countries that were part of the Empire were affected by it.

But between AD 400 and AD 500, the central control of the Empire collapsed. The countries that had been part of the Empire were left to go their own way. They were no longer defended by Roman armies or run by Roman Governors. **War** broke out between these countries. Britain was invaded by the tribes of the Angles and the Saxons. Rome itself was overrun by Barbarian tribes.

This had an impact on medicine:

- **Public health systems** that the Romans had built were destroyed.
- **Libraries** full of medical books were destroyed.
- The invading tribes did not know how to read, and so they **weren't interested in education** or the works of Galen.
- **War** was now the most important priority, and money was spent on armies rather than education and medicine.

The only powerful centralised body that survived the collapse of the Roman Empire was its religion – **the Christian Church**.

> **Revision task**
>
> Start to create your factor chart for the Middle Ages (see pages 12–13) using your knowledge and the notes in this topic.

The impact of Christianity and Islam on medicine

After the collapse of the Roman Empire, Christianity remained the main religion in Europe. Christian attitudes both helped and hindered the development of medicine in the Middle Ages.

Revision task

The Christian Church controlled education, which took place in monasteries. The training of doctors was banned Until AD 1100 but allowed after that. So, should it go in the 'helped' or 'hindered' column?

Christian attitudes	
Helped the development of medicine	**Hindered the development of medicine**
• As Jesus said in his teachings, Christians had **a religious duty to care for the sick**, which they did mainly in hospitals found in monasteries and nunneries. • The Christian Church **preserved, translated and copied many medical books** including those written by Galen and other Greek and Roman medical writers.	• The Christian Church **banned dissection**. • The Christian Church believed that **ancient writings should not be questioned** – if Galen was questioned people might also start questioning the Bible! • The Christian Church **supported Galen's and Hippocrates' ideas** because they fitted the idea that one God created all humans. • The Christian Church taught that **all illness was sent as a punishment from God**. It was right for the person to suffer and cures should only come from God.

In the seventh century, the new religion of Islam emerged in **the Arab world**. Islamic attitudes both helped and hindered the development of medicine in the Middle Ages.

Key term

The Arab world – countries in the Middle East and in North Africa

Islamic attitudes	
Helped the development of medicine	**Hindered the development of medicine**
• Followers of Islam had **a religious duty to care for the sick**, mainly in Arab hospitals. • The Arab rulers believed it was **important to develop education**. Islamic scholars **translated medical books** including books by Galen and other Greek medical writers. • **Arab doctors like al-Razi (Rhazes) and Ibn Sina (Avicenna) wrote books on medicine**, much of which was copied from the theories of Hippocrates and Galen, but they did also write about their own observations and ideas.	• The Islamic religion **banned dissection** because of its belief in the afterlife. • The Islamic religion **supported Galen's and Hippocrates' ideas** because they fitted the idea that Allah created humans as the parts of the body fit together perfectly.

Revision task

There were many similarities and differences between Islamic and Christian attitudes towards medicine. Use the information in the tables above to copy and complete this Venn diagram.

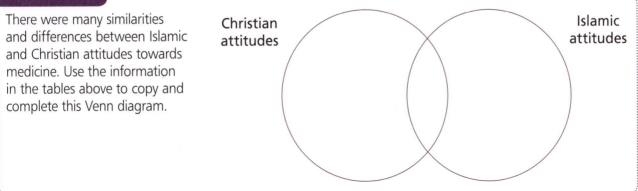

Christian attitudes · Islamic attitudes

The reasons for the acceptance of Galenic medicine

Revised ☐

People in the Middle Ages believed everything that Galen had written about medicine. They still believed in almost everything that the Greeks and Romans had believed in – **the theory of the four humours, the clinical method of observation** and **Galen's ideas about anatomy**.

Why was this?

It was mainly because of **religion. The Christian Church** was very powerful and it supported Galen's ideas because it fitted with the religious idea that God created humans and all parts of the human body worked perfectly together.

The Church did not allow people to disagree with these beliefs and nobody dared to question them. So people accepted Galen's ideas, and didn't challenge them. So healers in the Middle Ages still used treatments used by the Romans and still believed in the theory of the four humours. New ideas were discouraged.

Key term

Galenic medicine – everything that Galen wrote about medicine

Examiner's tip

If you are asked a question about why the theories of Galen and Hippocrates (such as the theory of the four humours) lasted such a long time, remember that it wasn't because the medicine worked brilliantly – but because **nobody challenged their ideas**.

The continuation of supernatural beliefs and treatments

Revised ☐

Although the Greeks and Romans had believed in observation and looking for natural explanations of illness, people in the Middle Ages were discouraged from using science to explain disease. **The Christian Church** was a strong influence on people and they encouraged **supernatural and superstitious** explanations of why people got ill.

One main belief was that God sent illness to people as punishment for their sins so only God could cure them. One main 'treatment' was therefore to pray to God for forgiveness.

However, like all the ancient civilisations, people living in the Middle Ages combined **natural** and **supernatural** explanations and treatments for illness. This is dramatically illustrated in the way that medieval people responded to a dreadful disease, the Black Death. This is covered in detail in the case study on page 34 but here is a summary of the main explanations and treatments at the time.

Natural explanations	Supernatural explanations
• **Bad air** and bad smells • When **the four humours** were out of balance • **Poisons** in the air • Minority groups, for example the Jews, were believed to have **poisoned wells** in Germany	• **Astrology** – the position of the stars and the earth and the signs of the zodiac • **God punishing** people for their sins • **The Devil** causing mischief

Natural treatments	Supernatural treatments
• **Cleaning** up towns that smelled bad • **Purging** – by vomiting or defecation • **Bleeding** • The use of **opposites** • **Stopping practices** like the 'kiss of obedience', which was when knights would kiss their lords and promise to obey them • The use of **herbal remedies**, such as honey and plantain	• **Praying** for forgiveness • **Beating themselves** with a stick to punish themselves for their sins • Making **gigantic candles** to burn in church 

Revision task

Here is a list of beliefs that people in the Middle Ages had about medicine. Are they natural or supernatural?

• Illness is caused when the four humours are out of balance.
• The jaw has two bones.

• Clinical observation can help find out more (especially looking at a patient's urine).
• God makes you ill because you have sinned.
• Blood is made in the liver.
• Shaving a chicken's bottom cures the plague (after you have strapped it to your boils).

Exam practice

1. Explain why religious beliefs were used to explain illness in the Middle Ages. **[7]**

Answers online

Examiner's tip

When you get an exam question like question 1 that asks you why medieval people had supernatural/religious explanations for the causes and treatments of illnesses, remember it **wasn't** because medieval people were stupid! It was because no individuals during this time had new ideas that led to great changes in medicine.

But why didn't people come up with ideas?

• People were concerned with wars, not with medicine.

• People weren't even **allowed** to come up with any new ideas because of the Church!

KQ See page 40 for key questions.

Case study: The Black Death in England

Revised

One of the most dramatic events in the history of medicine happened in the Middle Ages – the **Black Death**. It tells us quite a lot about what medicine was like in the Middle Ages, particularly what people thought caused disease and how they tried to treat it.

Causes of the Black Death

The Black Death started in China and came to Europe in 1348. Once it had arrived, it spread quickly from place to place.

The people of the Middle Ages did not know what had caused the disease. However, today the favourite explanation is that there were two plagues, the **bubonic** and the **pneumonic**.

> **Examiner's tip**
>
> You might get asked questions about this case study in either the Development Study paper or the Source Investigation.

Bubonic plague

- People were **infected by flea bites** from fleas that had previously bitten infected rats.
- Victims felt **cold** and tired.
- **Buboes** (painful swellings) appeared under the arms or in the groin – often as big as apples. Think of the biggest spot ever! As these buboes were filled with pus, they would burst, which caused blood poisoning. If it doesn't make you feel too ill, think about the colour of pus – which of the four humours would the medieval people think was to blame?
- Blisters appeared all over the body, followed by high fever, severe headaches, unconsciousness and (very often) **death after 4–7 days.**

Pneumonic plague

- This disease attacked the **lungs** and was more lethal than the bubonic plague.
- Victims would **cough up blood!** (What would the medieval humour expert think of this?)
- People were **infected by other people** who had the plague coughing over them.
- Victims **died** quickly, within **a day or two**.

By the end of 1349, one in three people had died of the Black Death in Europe. In London probably half the population – 50,000 people – died.

Responses to the Black Death

People were terrified of the Black Death. Think about other epidemics that have happened in the late twentieth century such as AIDS or swine flu. At least we had some idea of why and how those happened. Medieval people couldn't understand where it was coming from or why it was happening, and therefore what would stop it. They **did not have the scientific understanding** or the technology which would have shown them that it was germs from fleas on rats.

People **blamed the Black Death on various things** including: bad air and bad smells, the stars and planets, minority groups such as the Jews poisoning water, God punishing people for their sins, imbalance of the four humours, poor living conditions and dirty towns. Remember that blaming the Jews was not unique to the Black Death: they were traditionally used as scapegoats.

Some of their responses did help, for example cleaning streets or burning clothes. **Others did not**, such as putting shaved dead chickens on buboes.

Exam practice

1. Study Source A. What does it tell you about what people in the Middle Ages believed about the Black Death? **[6]**

Source A: *A fourteenth-century picture about the Black Death showing people burning the clothes of victims of the Black Death*

Answers online

1.8 The Middle Ages (2): Surgery, living conditions and caring for the ill

You saw from the previous topic that the Middle Ages was mostly a time of continuity. Galen's ideas continued to be used to explain disease and to decide how to treat it. However, there were ways in which medical care was changing.

> ## Key content
> - Developments in surgery
> - Living conditions and health and hygiene
> - Domestic medicine, childbirth and the role of women
> - Hospitals and caring for the ill
> - Case study: Public health in the Middle Ages

Developments in surgery

Revised ☐

War was common in the Middle Ages. People got **injured in battle**, and **barber surgeons** developed new ways of treating them. Barber surgeons were not trained doctors, but they conducted operations such as removing teeth. They were the ones who did the most surgery on the battlefields and they had many methods which helped their patients, such as using wine as an antiseptic. However, doctors looked down on the barber surgeons because they had not been trained at university (and so by the Church).

Operations were very dangerous as infections were common and infection could lead to death. They were only carried out when necessary, such as amputating a very badly damaged limb, or removing an arrow.

Christian barber surgeons are sometimes compared to the Muslim doctors who treated soldiers during the **Crusades**. Muslim doctors did not operate as often as Christian surgeons, and they were careful to keep the wound clean to help prevent infection.

> ### Key terms
>
> **Barber surgeon** – a barber (of the haircut variety) who also provided medical help including small operations like tooth extraction
>
> **Crusades** – in the Middle Ages Christians from Europe fought the Muslim Turks for control of the Holy Land

> ### Examiner's tip
>
> If you are asked about how medicine developed in the Middle Ages, remember that surgery is the **only** area which saw some progress. This was mainly because lots of people were wounded in battles and so doctors had to improve their methods or those people would not be able to fight any more.

Living conditions and health and hygiene

Revised ☐

Living conditions and health and hygiene were pretty bad in the Middle Ages, particularly in **towns**:

- Towns were cramped and streets were narrow.
- Human waste went into the streets, and into the streams where people got their drinking water.
- Wells for drinking water were often close to cesspools of sewage.
- Even in the **villages**, people lived in smoke-filled huts that they also shared with animals in winter.

You can find out more about this in the public health case study on pages 38–39.

Monks and nuns, who lived in **monasteries and nunneries**, generally had better living conditions, with fresh water and toilets. Most monasteries were wealthy so they could afford to keep themselves healthy, clean and well-fed.

Domestic medicine, childbirth and the role of women

Revised

Medicine in the home was the job of the women. Most villages would have a **wise woman**, who would act as the midwife, and make **natural remedies** for general aches and pains that were not cured quickly. Treatments like this were generally effective, as some of the plants, for example onions and lichen, and substances taken from animals contained natural antibiotics, although the people in the Middle Ages didn't know *why* they worked.

Most men kept well away from involvement in childbirth, although a few were starting to take an interest. **Midwives** assisted in the delivery, passing on their methods through the generations of women.

However, the **Church did not encourage women to take an active role in medicine**. They saw women as inferior to men. They were happy for women to look after their families at home, but disapproved of the wise women. The Church sometimes accused wise women of witchcraft!

Nuns did look after sick people in nunneries, but women were not allowed to train as doctors in the universities (which were run by the Church).

Hospitals and caring for the ill

Revised

Monasteries and nunneries were important centres of religion where monks and nuns dedicated their lives to God. This involved praying, reading the Bible, and also caring for the sick.

Many had a separate hospital for the public, run by monks or nuns. It was their **religious duty to care for the sick**. Treatments in these hospitals involved eating a particular diet and sleeping well, as well as balancing the four humours. There was lots of praying too, asking God for his forgiveness.

Barber surgeons did not work at these hospitals, and so operations were not very common.

Hospitals did not have to admit someone who had an infectious disease. Not many monks died during the Black Death as they cut themselves off from society in their monasteries rather than taking in victims. However, many of the parish priests *did* die, because they cared for the sick in their parish.

In a similar way, **Islamic hospitals** were encouraged by the Islamic religion. They had different wards for different diseases. They would also support patients when they were getting better after they left the hospital.

> **Revision task**
>
> Complete your factor chart for the Middle Ages (see pages 12–13) using your knowledge and the notes in this topic.

Case study: Public health in the Middle Ages

In Roman times England had good public health systems. But these systems were destroyed after the collapse of the Roman Empire. In the Middle Ages towns in England were unhealthy places.

However, people did try to find ways to improve them. Kings and town officials passed laws to clean up towns. However they were hard to enforce. There were only a small number of officials trying to enforce the laws, and not enough to punish everyone who broke them.

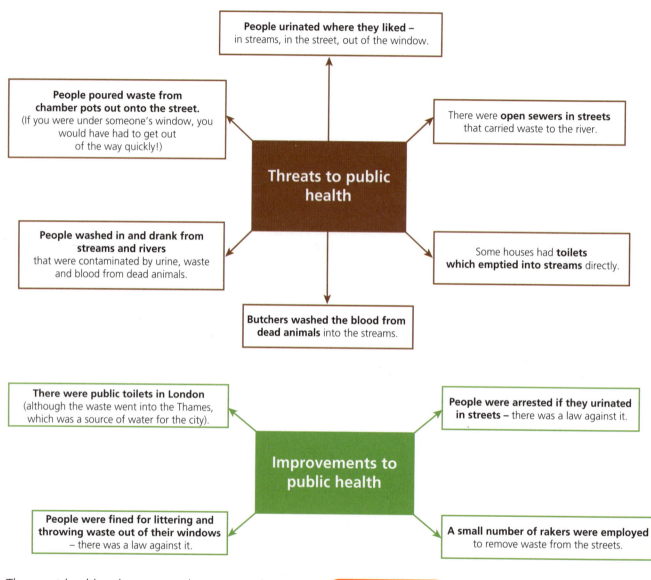

The most healthy places were the monasteries because:

- They were **located near fresh water** and had toilets.
- They were **rich and well organised**.
- Monks believed that **being clean was part of worshipping God**.

Common question-type 2

Another common type of question in the Source Investigation is about 'proof'. For example:

- Does Source A prove that people at the time believed…?
- Does Source B prove that Source C was wrong about…?

Be very careful when you are asked questions about proof! 'Prove' is a very strong word in history as we are often unable to prove anything without argument. So the question is inviting you to use

- your background knowledge, and
- the other sources on the paper

to say whether the source is **typical** (representative). It also wants you to

- think about reliability (even if a source is typical, do you trust the source to tell you the truth?)
- be balanced and careful.

And remember, one source on its own proves nothing. It could be one person's opinion and everyone else at the time might have had a different opinion. For example, Source A could be a law that nobody paid any attention to.

Exam practice

1. Does Source A prove that people in the Middle Ages believed in natural causes of disease? **[9]**

Source A: *Letter from King Edward III to the Lord Mayor of London 1349*

'You are to make sure that all the human excrement and other filth lying in the street of the city is removed. You are to cause the city to be cleaned from all bad smells so that no more people will die from such smells.'

Source B: *Detail from a fourteenth-century work called* Omne Bonum, *showing people with the plague being blessed by a priest*

How to answer this question:

1. **Read**. Examine Source A closely. Does it show belief in natural causes of disease?

2. **Compare** with your background knowledge. What do you know about this? Is this source typical of its time?

3. **Cross-reference** with the other sources on this paper (here there is only one other but in the exam there will be several). Does Source B show a natural or a supernatural belief about disease?

4. **Read the caption**. Who made or wrote the source? What was their purpose? Do you trust them to tell the truth?

5. **Write**. Then you are ready to write about the source. Include **examples** from the source that back up what you are saying.

NB This is a 9-mark question so allow about 15 minutes.

Exam practice

1. Briefly describe the part played by monasteries in medicine in the Middle Ages. **[5]**

2. 'Religion had more impact than government did on medicine in the Middle Ages.' How for do you agree with this statement? **[8]**

Answers online

KQ

Key question	Medicine in the Middle Ages
What caused people to be healthy or unhealthy?	– Injuries from fighting in battles – Poor hygiene in cramped towns – Plagues such as the Black Death
Who provided medical care?	– Women in homes, wise women, midwives for childbirth – Barber surgeons – Monks and nuns in monasteries and other religious hospitals – Doctors for the rich
What ideas did people have about the **causes** and **treatments** of illness and injuries?	**Causes:** *natural* – bad air and smells, imbalance of the four humours *supernatural* – sent by God as punishment, astrology **Treatments:** *natural* – use of opposites and four humours (bleeding, purging), herbal remedies *supernatural* – praying to God for forgiveness, self-beating
What caused diagnoses and treatments to remain the same or to change?	Very little change during this time due to the impact of war and religion
How far did new ideas and treatments affect the majority of the population?	– The majority carried on with herbal remedies and used ideas from Hippocrates and Galen – There were some advances in the treatment of war wounds

1.9 The medical Renaissance

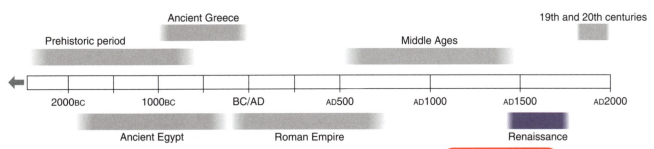

'Renaissance' literally means 'rebirth'. In history, it means **the rebirth of Greek and Roman** attitudes of observation, enquiry and investigation. The Ancient Greeks and Romans, such as Hippocrates and Galen, had tried to think for themselves. This attitude was rediscovered and helped to change medicine.

> ## Key content
>
> - The rebirth of Greek ideas of careful observation of nature
> - Vesalius and advances in knowledge of anatomy
> - Paré and developments in surgery
> - Harvey and developments in physiology
> - The extent of the impact of these developments on the medical treatment of the majority of the population
> - The growth of a medical profession
> - The reduced role of women in professional medicine
> - Case study: Quack doctors
> - Case study: Inoculation, Jenner and the development of vaccination

The rebirth of Greek ideas of careful observation of nature

 Revised

Hippocrates and Galen wrote in Greek and Latin. In the Middle Ages, the books that they wrote were kept in libraries, but only religious scholars were allowed to see and translate them. If these scholars saw something in the book they were copying that they did not believe in, they would simply not copy that part. For example, Galen wrote that his ideas should be checked by human dissection. Because the scholars didn't believe in dissection, they didn't copy this bit across and so this opinion was not spread.

The original books written by Hippocrates and Galen were rediscovered in the fifteenth century. Renaissance thinkers wanted to read and translate the **original** books – and when they did, they found that there were lots of changes that had been made by the scholars, such as taking out the bit about human dissection. People like Vesalius looked at these works and wanted to question the old medieval ideas by dissecting humans.

Artists like Leonardo da Vinci began to **look closely at nature**, and to copy what they saw. This included studying the **detail of the human body**, which improved their knowledge of anatomy.

Examiner's tip

Renaissance people 'rediscovered' but also 'challenged' Galen. You need to understand that they rediscovered Galen's **attitude not his facts**. Galen himself had said people should check his findings by doing dissections. By following Galen's attitudes of observation and experimentation, they actually proved that some of his findings were wrong. But that is not a contradiction. It is how science works.

Revision task

Start to create your factor chart for Renaissance Medicine (see pages 12–13). There is plenty in the tables on pages 42–43 to guide you. Look for religion, war, science and technology, and communication.

Examiner's tip

Picture sources from the Renaissance look much more like what we find in the natural world today than the pictures from the Middle Ages. They drew from nature on purpose, as this was what the Greeks and Romans had done. Make sure you remember to include this point if you are asked questions in the exam about sources from these two time periods.

Revision task

1. In Renaissance medicine you need to know about: Vesalius, Paré (pronounced Pa-ray) and Harvey. Use the information here and a chart like this to summarise their contributions to medicine.

Name	Theory	How found: by chance or experiment?	Who/What did he prove wrong?
Vesalius			
Paré			
Harvey			

2. Create your social network profiles for the three individuals, using the guidance on page 4.

Examiner's tip

You need to be clear about which **old ideas** each man changed:

● **Vesalius** proved **Galen** wrong about **anatomy**. This led to other ideas by other Greek and Roman thinkers being challenged.

● **Paré** proved the **old ideas** about **surgery** were wrong.

● **Harvey** challenged the **theory of the four humours** and proved **Galen** was wrong about **how blood was made**.

Vesalius and advances in knowledge of anatomy

Revised

	Name: Vesalius **Dates of discoveries: 1530s–1560s**
Education and career	Studied medicine in France and in Padua, Italy. In Padua, students were urged to look closely at nature (as the Greek and Roman books had told them to do). Became professor of surgery in Padua.
Ideas	● Vesalius looked closely at nature. To take a closer look at the human body, he robbed cemeteries to get bodies to dissect. This wasn't as uncommon at the time as we might think. ● In 1543, Vesalius wrote a book called *The Fabric of the Human Body*. This described how the body worked, and included very detailed pictures by the Renaissance artist Titian. ● Vesalius wrote that Galen's theories of anatomy were wrong and gave examples: a) The jaw was made from one bone, not two; b) The breastbone had three parts, not seven; c) He found out that women had the same number of ribs as men – which questioned the Bible story where Adam gave up one of his ribs to make Eve (and therefore men had one less rib). ● Vesalius showed that doctors could learn so much through human dissection. ● The Church was horrified at what Vesalius was writing! Other students read Vesalius' work and started to question Greek and Roman medical ideas, as well as the teachings of the Church.
How did he achieve what he did?	Before Vesalius a few other doctors had questioned what Galen had said – even Galen himself had written that his ideas needed to be checked by dissection. Vesalius' work happened at the same time as the invention of the **printing press** and as artists became interested in drawing details direct from nature. This meant that his ideas and illustrations were **printed in books** and **spread** all over Europe to people who would not be able (or want) to watch live dissections.
BUT ...	● Nobody was healthier as a result of Vesalius' work. ● Many doctors refused to accept that Galen could be wrong and continued to dissect only animals or to read the old books.

Paré and developments in surgery

	Name: Paré　　　**Dates of discoveries: 1530s–1560s**
Education and career	Learned surgery as an apprentice to his brother. He was a barber surgeon, and not considered a 'proper' doctor by those trained at university. He was a surgeon with the French army from 1536 to 1556 and then became surgeon to kings of France. NB although Paré had not been to university, he had read Greek and Roman medical works, and used them as the basis of his new treatments.
Ideas	**Idea 1 Treating wounds:** In wartime, many soldiers were injured in battles, where guns and cannons were widely used. Gunshot wounds were new, and to treat them surgeons poured boiling oil onto the wound. Paré **ran out of oil**, so he made up his own version of an old Roman method of healing which used a poultice made of egg yolk, turpentine and other cold oils. The next morning, those who were treated with this new method were sitting up and feeling better.
	Idea 2 Stopping bleeding: If a soldier lost a limb in a battle (more common than you might think), the stump would bleed. Surgeons stopped the bleeding by using a **cautering iron** (a red hot piece of metal) to seal the blood vessels. Paré used silk thread to tie **ligatures** around arteries, a different way of stopping the bleeding.
	More ideas! Paré wrote two books, *Works on Surgery* and *Apology and Treatise*, relating his new theories and other ideas, such as the use of artificial limbs and even an artificial nose!
How did he achieve what he did?	Partly by chance, as he tried out his Roman-style poultice because he ran out of boiling oil. Printing his books helped to spread his ideas quickly. Paré learned from experience, not just from reading books.
BUT ...	Although Paré's methods were less shocking to the human body than hot oil or cauterising, they still sometimes killed people because of the infections that occurred. It was not until **antiseptics** were discovered in the late 1800s that Paré's ideas could be used widely and safely.

Harvey and developments in physiology

	Name: Harvey　　　**Dates of discoveries: 1620s–1650s**
Education and career	Studied medicine at Cambridge University. Moved to Padua in 1600 to carry on his training. Returned to London as a qualified doctor. Became a famous doctor to James I and Charles I.
Ideas	**Harvey's most important idea** was about how blood circulated in the body. Previously, people had believed Galen's theory that new blood was made in the liver to replace blood that was burned up in the body. This meant that they believed you could have too much blood and have an imbalance in your humours. This was the reason for blood letting – the most common treatment based on the four humours theory.
	Harvey did experiments to prove that the heart was like a pump – that it circulated the same blood around the body. He did this through:
	● experimenting on living people – this showed that there were valves in the veins and that blood could flow only one way
	● showing others how his theory worked by drawing detailed illustrations
	● his book, *An Anatomical Account of the Motion of the Heart and Blood*, which proved his point and spread his ideas.
	Harvey's ideas were a direct challenge to one of the most basic treatments – bleeding. If blood was continually circulating, the body couldn't be making too much blood, so bleeding was irrelevant or, worse still, dangerous.
How did he achieve what he did?	Through experiments which involved careful dissection and observation of detail.
BUT ...	Harvey's ideas could not be immediately proved without argument, as they needed proof that there were tiny blood vessels which took the blood to every part of the body. But they can't be seen with the human eye. Harvey needed the invention of better microscopes to prove this final bit of his theory. He died before this happened.

The extent of the impact of these developments on the medical treatment of the majority of the population

Revised

In the short term, these developments had no impact on treatments. Look at the 'BUT...' section in each profile on pages 42–43. Most people carried on using herbal remedies, visiting wise women and midwives, along with using treatments such as bleeding, which was based on the theory of the four humours. The plague of 1665 in England saw the use of supernatural treatments that are almost as weird and wacky as those of the Black Death:

- writing abracadabra backwards and forwards
- smoking tobacco
- Paré recommended wearing a lucky charm
- putting the bottom of a chicken onto the buboes!

However, at least this time people were isolated by the authorities putting crosses on the doors of houses where people were sick.

But in the long term (well after their deaths) these men's discoveries and their scientific methods led to new treatments such as: stitches, blood transfusion, artificial limbs and medical students dissecting bodies as part of their training.

> ### Examiner's tip
> Have some of these remedies ready to use in your exam as examples of old treatments carrying on after the time of Vesalius, Paré and Harvey.

> ### Examiner's tip
> For question 1 here, in your first paragraph write what you know about what the individual did.
>
> Then, explain the impact. Think about not what the individual **did** but about what their work **did** or **didn't** change in medicine, in the short term and long term.

> ### Exam practice
>
> 1. Explain why Harvey is important in the history of medicine. **[7]**
>
> 2. Explain why Paré was able to make advances in medicine. **[7]**
>
> 3. 'Vesalius is more important than Harvey in the history of medicine.' How far do you agree with this statement? **[8]**
>
> **Answers online**

> ### Examiner's tip
> - When you answer questions like question 3, you need to look at each individual in turn and consider what they **changed**, both in the short term and in the long term.
>
> - To get the highest mark you need to come to a conclusion. It **does not matter** what that conclusion is, as long as it is supported by historical knowledge.

The growth of a medical profession

Revised

The increasing use of scientific method in medicine helped change the role and reputation of doctors.

- Doctors were **trained at universities** around Europe. For example, Harvey trained at the famous university of Padua in Italy.
- Doctors (or physicians as they were known then) regarded themselves as **professional and expert** and tried to improve their methods of treatment by learning from others. Some, such as Edward Jenner (see page 48), made great steps forward in using scientific method to improve treatments.
- They also tried to protect their reputation by **preventing untrained people** from practising as doctors. For example, the main job of the Royal College of Physicians in England (set up in the sixteenth century) was to register and license doctors and to prevent unqualified people from practising.

The reduced role of women in professional medicine

Revised

All professional doctors were men! **Women could not train as doctors** or go to universities. Professional medical care was taken over by men. The Renaissance also changed the role of women in other ways.

- **The decline of the wise woman:** in the Middle Ages, every village had a wise woman who provided medical help, herbal cures and delivered babies. In the 1600s many wise women were accused of being witches, which discouraged women from offering medical care beyond their family.
- **Male doctors became more and more involved in childbirth** – particularly for the rich. It became 'trendy' for rich women to have a professional doctor to attend to their birth rather than a traditional midwife.
- When childbirth became more 'scientific' (for example in the **use of forceps** to deliver babies) doctors forbade women to use these methods. Only male doctors could use forceps. This further reduced the role of the female midwife for richer people.

However, women still cared for their family at home. Many read books that were available to improve their skills and their cures.

Revision task

List one change affecting each of these aspects of medicine in the Medieval Renaissance:
- training of doctors
- childbirth
- role of wise women.

KQ

Key question	Medicine in the Renaissance
What caused people to be healthy or unhealthy?	– Injuries in battle – Plagues – one particularly bad plague struck in 1665 (but don't confuse this with the Black Death) – Infectious diseases such as smallpox
Who provided medical care?	– Women in the home, wise women, midwives for childbirth – Barber surgeons – Monks in monasteries and other religious hospitals – Doctors for the rich (doctors like Harvey) – Quack doctors
What ideas did people have about the **causes** and **treatments** of illness and injuries?	**Causes:** *natural* – imbalance of the four humours *supernatural* – illnesses sent by God as punishment **Treatments:** *natural* – use of opposites and four humours (bleeding, purging), herbal remedies *supernatural* – praying to God for forgiveness
What caused diagnoses and treatments to remain the same or to change?	Treatments for illnesses stayed the same because new ideas like those of Vesalius and Harvey were about understanding the body not about new treatments. There were some advances in treatment of war wounds, especially in France with Paré
How far did new ideas and treatments affect the majority of the population?	Very little in the short term; the majority continued with herbal remedies and ideas from Galen

Case study: Quack doctors

There were not many doctors and it cost a lot to see them so professional doctors were really **only for the rich**. There were also:

- **apothecaries**, who made and sold medicines and remedies. They also gave advice to people who visited them.
- **barber surgeons**, who did basic operations. Paré was a barber surgeon but most were not nearly as skilled as him.
- **quacks** – untrained people who sold medicines.

What were quacks?

Quack is short for quacksalver. Originally the word applied to anyone who sold medicines on the street. Later 'quack' or 'quackery' became an insult towards almost any mistrusted doctor or healer. There were quacks in England from the 1650s to the early 1800s although the focus of this case study is the mid-eighteenth century.

The original quacks were much like market or fairground traders. They were totally untrained. They took their supposed 'miracle cures' from town to town. They attracted customers to their stall with music and a clown or a monkey and shouting. They often claimed to have travelled from other countries and brought back their medicine. They said their remedies were made from secret ingredients and were a 'miracle' cure for almost any ailment.

What did the trained doctors think?

In the 1700s as doctors became more professional and better trained they got increasingly worried about quacks. The professionals said the quacks were worthless or dangerous. University trained doctors saw quacks as conmen and as competition rather than allies.

- **Doctors thought quacks were often not very good at being doctors**. Quack remedies could be useless or sometimes fatal.
- **Quacks took business away from professional doctors,** which meant that the doctors lost money.
- **Quacks undermined the reputation** of the whole medical profession – patients did not know how to tell a trained doctor from an untrained one.

So why did people buy their medicines?

Despite the opposition of the professional doctors, quacks and their remedies flourished. Partly this is because the trained doctors were expensive. Most quacks were only out to make money but their medicines were cheaper than a visit to the doctor. Poor people could not afford to see a doctor so, if they were ill, what else could they do? Also, if ordinary people did not understand the causes of disease, they had no way of knowing whether pills or potions would be any good. We know that even today when people are ill they will try almost anything in the hope it will work.

> **Examiner's tip**
>
> You might get asked questions about quack doctors in either the Development Study paper or the Source Investigation.

> **Examiner's tip**
>
> **Sources about quacks**
>
> Quacks were common but also controversial. Sources range from quacks advertising their miracle cures to doctors complaining about the quacks' medicines or their methods. There are cartoons or songs satirising the quacks. However there are also sources that show that not all quacks were as bad as each other.
>
> You need to pay particular attention to who has written or created a source – for example, is it by a doctor exposing the quacks, or by a quack explaining how good they are?

Common question-type 3

The Source Investigation will nearly always have a question about usefulness. For example:

- How useful is Source A for....?
- Which is more useful for..., Source A or Source B?

The two most important things to remember about usefulness are:

- A source is not useful or useless in itself. It is useful or useless for **finding out about a particular topic**. So you need to read the question carefully: useful… for what?
- It is closely linked to reliability. A source can only be useful for coming to a conclusion in an enquiry if you can trust it to be reliable on that subject. For example, in the exam practice question below you need to assess if either source is reliable in order to decide how useful it is for finding out about the reputation of quack doctors.

Exam practice

1. Which source is more useful for finding out about the reputation of quack doctors, Source A or Source B?
[8]

Source A: *From a folk play performed in the eighteenth century (folk plays make fun of people)*

'THE DOCTOR: In comes I, old Doctor Black –
                          Although I'm very old, still I can quack.
THE ADMIRAL: What can you cure?
THE DOCTOR: Anything.
                          If there is nine pins in a man's eye
                          I'll pull eleven out.
THE ADMIRAL: What will you cure this dead man for?
THE DOCTOR: A thousand pounds and a bottle of wine.'

Source B: *Some 'rules for identifying quacks', written by a doctor in 1767*

'1. Never trust those who pretend that the good of mankind is their only reason for offering their medicines for sale.

2. Conclude the advertiser to be a fool who pretends that his medicine will cure different illnesses which have no connection with each other.

3. Do not believe lists of cases where the medicine is said to have worked, these are usually invented by the quack.'

Answers online

Examiner's tip

How to answer this question:

1. Look at the **content** of the source. Does it tell you information that you need to know for your enquiry? Or does it miss out things that you think important?

2. **Cross-reference** with the other sources – here there is only one other but in the exam there will be several. Do they contain similar or different information?

3. Use your **background knowledge** to work out whether this source is **typical** or a one-off.

4. Evaluate the origin and purpose and reliability of the source. Do you trust it to tell the truth?

5. Then you are ready to **write** an answer. As always include **examples** from the source that back up what you are saying.

NB This is an 8-mark question so allow around 12–15 minutes.

Case study: Inoculation, Jenner and the development of vaccination

Revised ☐

In the eighteenth century, smallpox was a common, but **dreaded, killer disease** with no known cure. Those who survived were often **scarred for life**.

One way of preventing smallpox was **inoculation**.

- This was popularised in England by **Lady Mary Wortley Montague** after she had seen the practice being used in Turkey.

Examiner's tip

You might get asked questions about this case study in either the Development Study paper or the Source Investigation.

- It involved spreading a small amount of pus from a smallpox scab onto the skin of a healthy person. They got a minor case of smallpox which helped their body build up **immunity** to the real thing.
- **No one knew quite why it worked** but it was used very widely and successfully.
- However poor people could not afford inoculation. And sometimes it failed if the doctor got the dose wrong so the patient could get severe smallpox. **Some were reluctant** to be inoculated because they feared inoculation almost as much as they feared getting smallpox.

Edward Jenner: vaccination against smallpox

Edward Jenner discovered a much safer way to protect people against smallpox.

Jenner was a **doctor** working in the rural area of Gloucestershire. He had heard that dairymaids who had caught a mild disease called cowpox seemed to avoid catching smallpox. He was a member of the Royal Society (a group of scientists) and he knew that experiment was the way to make medical progress. He decided to test the connection between cowpox and smallpox to see if one disease prevented the other.

He injected a young boy called James Phipps with cowpox matter and later injected him again, this time with smallpox matter. James survived. Jenner repeated the test on a further 23 cases. All were successfully treated. He named this process **vaccination** after the Latin word 'vacca', meaning 'cow'.

Impact

His method was successful. His ideas spread quickly. And, unlike the other developments you have studied in earlier centuries, such as Harvey's work on the heart, they soon improved the health of ordinary people.

1798 Jenner published his findings
1802 Parliament granted Jenner £30,000 to continue his work
1803 Vaccination was also being used in the USA
1807 Parliament granted more money for Jenner's work
1852 Vaccination against smallpox was made compulsory in England.

Edward Jenner had introduced the first vaccination against disease. This was significant in the history of medicine, as it was a totally new idea to inject people with one disease in order to prevent them catching a different disease. This idea was the foundation of modern vaccinations.

Revision task

Create a five frame storyboard to summarise how Jenner developed the first vaccination. For example:

1. inoculation
2. cowpox/dairymaid
3. James Phipps experiment
4. other experiments
5. reaction of parliament.

The vaccination debate

Although Jenner worked carefully and scientifically and the method was successful, vaccination was controversial and Jenner faced a great deal of opposition.

Doctors who performed inoculation were worried about losing business and income. They also believed that inoculation was a tried method and wanted to stick with what they knew rather than trying out a new and unusual idea.	As a country doctor Jenner **was not respected by leading people** in the medical profession. He could not explain the science behind why it worked. When he first presented his findings the Royal Society refused to publish them.
Once vaccination was proved to work the government got behind it and made it compulsory but some people **thought it was not government's role** to get involved in such things. They set up an anti-vaccination society to fight against it.	Some religious people (and non-religious people) were appalled by the **unnatural idea of giving a human an animal disease**.

1.10 Overview timeline – the nineteenth and twentieth centuries

Fighting disease, surgery and public health | Revised ☐

1796 Jenner discovers smallpox vaccination

1832 Cholera epidemic

1842 Chadwick's report on public health

1847 Simpson discovers that chloroform can send patients to sleep

1848 First Public Health Act

1853 Smallpox vaccination compulsory

1854 Cholera epidemic: John Snow discovers that the disease is spread

1854 Crimean war: Florence Nightingale shows that clean hospitals

1857 Queen Victoria uses chloroform; until 1860s death rates from

1861 Pasteur germ theory

1865 Lister discovers and proves that carbolic acid can be used

1867 Poor people get the vote

1872 Koch begins investigating different germs which cause

1875 Public Health Act: towns must clean streets and sewers.

1879 Pasteur finds a vaccination for chicken cholera using

1890 Halstead suggests the use of rubber gloves

1900 Blood groups discovered by Landsteiner

1906–11 Liberal reforms

1911 First chemical compound (a 'magic

1914–18 Plastic surgery improved

1928 Fleming discovers that

1930s Fleming and Florey

1939–45 Penicillin

1948 NHS founded

1967

Key
☐ Fighting disease
☐ Surgery
☐ Public health

1800   1850   1900   1950

A lot happened in this period so as well as the overview timeline on pages 10–11 you will need a separate one for the nineteenth and twentieth centuries with more detail. The timeline here will get you started. It shows the key information relating to the three themes of:

● Fighting disease

● Surgery

● Public health

1. Each of the entries is colour coded. Decide which theme the entries are about then colour code the key.
2. As you revise the three topics, **either** add other dates and notes to this timeline **or**, better still, make your own much bigger timeline so there is room for your own notes, arrows (links) and drawings.

Examiner's tip

This period is divided by theme but the timeline will help you show the connections.

For example:

Pasteur's breakthrough in understanding disease

had a direct effect on

Lister's surgery

and on

the British government's attitude to public health

You can show these things by adding arrows linking events on the timeline. This will be useful for your exam: making connections like this is a good way to improve your marks.

in water

reduce deaths from infection

operations go up

to kill germs during operations

disease

Towns can charge taxes to do this

weak germs

during surgery

bullet') cures infection (syphilis)

because of wounds during the First World War

penicillin kills germs

develop penicillin

mass–produced because of Second World War

First heart transplant

1980s Deaths from AIDS (Acquired Immune Deficiency Syndrome) begin

2000

1.11 Fighting disease in the nineteenth and twentieth centuries

In the early 1800s ideas about the causes of disease were changing.

- Supernatural explanations and the theory of the four humours were no longer popular.
- The main belief in the early nineteenth century was that bad smells made you ill and spread disease – so people avoided bad smells to keep healthy. They believed **miasma** (an infected mist) rose out of things like rotting food and human waste in the street.
- Stronger microscopes had allowed people to see tiny micro-organisms (**bacteria**) in food, water and human waste. The big question was – how were they connected with disease?

The miasma theory was not right but it was closer to the truth than the theory of the four humours, and the second half of the nineteenth century saw decisive progress in understanding and treating disease.

Key term

miasma – smells from decomposing material that were believed to cause disease

bacteria – another word for micro-organisms or germs

Key content

- Pasteur and the development of the germ theory of disease
- Koch and developments in bacteriology
- Developments in drugs and vaccines
- Case study: The development of penicillin
- Case study: The development of hospitals
- The battle against infectious and non-infectious disease in the twentieth century

Pasteur and the development of the germ theory of disease

Revised

Louis Pasteur was a chemist who worked in France. In 1857 he was asked by wine producers to find out why their alcohol went sour.

- Using microscopes, he discovered that germs were **making** the alcohol go sour.
- He discovered that this also happened in milk and beer!
- He found out that if any liquid was heated, the germs were killed. So from then on the brewers did this. This process was called **pasteurisation**. We still use it today for milk to stop it going bad so quickly.

Pasteur had proved a link between germs in beer and the beer going bad. The germs cause the problem. He now made an important connection. If this happened in wine, beer or milk could it also happen in animals and humans? Could it be that **germs cause disease in the human body** in the same way? He published this germ theory of disease in **1861**.

Not everyone was convinced. They still believed in miasma (bad air causing disease) and 'spontaneous generation' (decay creating germs rather than the other way round) so in **1864** Pasteur set out to prove his theories through a series of experiments.

Examiner's tip

Pasteur is a great example to use for the factor of **individual genius**. He was a unique character: a scientist and a showman. Because he had proved the germ theory **scientifically** (another factor there), he was so convinced that it was true that he was prepared to stand up in public and demonstrate his idea.

Koch and developments in bacteriology

Revised

Koch was a German doctor who had read Pasteur's work and studied bacteria.

- In **1872**, Koch discovered that he could dye (stain) germs, and by doing so he could identify which germs caused which diseases.
- He identified the germs which caused different diseases: **anthrax** in **1872**, **tuberculosis** (TB) in **1882**, and **cholera** in **1883**.

Developments in drugs and vaccines

Revised

Once the link had been made between germs and disease it was a question of isolating each germ and then finding a way to treat it. Through the 1880s they made a series of breakthroughs.

Pasteur: an accidental discovery

Pasteur was experimenting with chicken cholera. He used Koch's methods to identify which bacteria were causing the disease. When he injected chickens with these germs they got chicken cholera and died.

Then chance intervened! His assistant left a batch of chicken cholera germs exposed to the air while he was away on holiday. When he returned he used this stale batch and the chickens did not die. However when they gave the same chickens the full dose of germs from a new batch, the chickens survived that too!

Pasteur worked out that the weakened germs had protected the chickens from the disease. He knew all about Jenner's work on smallpox 75 years earlier and in honour of Jenner he called this way of preventing disease 'vaccination' (even though it had nothing to do with cows).

Other vaccinations

Once Pasteur knew how this worked he developed vaccinations against other diseases.

- In 1881 a vaccination against anthrax in animals
- In 1882 his first vaccination for humans – against rabies.

However…Pasteur's work on vaccination could only prevent disease. What about actually curing people who had already got a disease?

Koch and Erlich: magic bullets to kill germs

The next step was taken by Koch and his team who investigated how to kill the germs when a person was already ill.

- In 1909, Koch's assistant, Paul **Ehrlich**, began to search for a chemical compound that would kill a particular germ in the body but not the person who had the disease. They already knew how to stain bacteria. How about if this stain was something that actually attacked and killed the bacteria? Ehrlich called this a **magic bullet** as it would go straight to the harmful bacteria to kill it.
- In **1911** the first magic bullet was discovered: Salvarsan 606, which cured syphilis.
- Gerhard **Domagk** went on to develop a magic bullet to cure blood poisoning. This was made from the chemical **sulphonamide**. Unfortunately, it also attacked the kidneys and liver so was not used unless someone was very, very ill.

Case study: The development of penicillin

Revised

Examiner's tip

You might get asked questions about this case study in either the Development Study paper or the Source Investigation.

Key terms

Antibiotic – a drug used to treat infections caused by bacteria, e.g. penicillin. Taken internally

Antiseptic – a chemical used to destroy bacteria and prevent infection. Used externally

The next really important development was the discovery of penicillin. This was like a magic bullet but, unlike Salversan 606 which was a chemical, penicillin was a naturally occurring mould. So it was a new kind of treatment – using one kind of helpful organism to fight a harmful one. This kind of drug is called an **antibiotic**. This is how it happened.

Stage 1: Alexander Fleming discovers the power of penicillin – by accident

In 1928 Fleming was one of many scientists trying to find ways of treating severe infections such as blood poisoning. One day, he went off on holiday and did not do his washing up. He left petri dishes with bacteria in them on his lab bench. He came back to discover that a mould called penicillin was growing in the petri dish, and this **mould had killed the bacteria all around it**! (NB Fleming was not the first person to have identified this mould. Joseph **Lister** had done so in 1872 but had not taken it further.)

- Fleming experimented with using the mould as an **antiseptic** (i.e. on the outside of the body).
- He **wrote up his findings** in a report but nobody thought it was important at the time.

Stage 2: Howard Florey and Ernest Chain turn penicillin into a treatment

Florey and Chain read Fleming's report in the 1930s. They started experimenting with it. They worked out a way to turn the mould into an **antibiotic** which could be injected into the body.

They proved it worked on animals then did a human trial on a policeman who had blood poisoning. They treated the infection for five days and he quickly got better. But then they ran out of penicillin and the policeman fell ill again and died.

They could see it worked but they needed to find a way to mass produce it and that needed money which they did not have.

Stage 3: The Second World War and mass production

Florey travelled to America to see if they would fund mass production. In 1942 the **Second World War** was raging. Wounded soldiers needed protection from blood poisoning and other infections and illnesses. The US government saw the potential for penicillin and paid for it to be mass produced. By 1944 there was enough penicillin to treat all the soldiers injured in the D-Day invasions.

Meanwhile, also in 1942, Fleming obtained some penicillin from Florey and used it to treat his friend who was dying of meningitis in St Mary's Hospital, London. When the friend recovered, the hospital told the press and almost overnight Fleming and penicillin were famous.

Examiner's tip

Penicillin is a **great** example of a range of factors affecting medical progress.

- **Chance**: Fleming not doing the washing up and finding penicillin in his petri dishes. (Does this remind you of anyone else? Pasteur's assistant perhaps? See page 53.)
- **Science and technology**: experiments – Fleming on killing germs and Florey on humans.
- **Government**: the US government funding the mass production of penicillin because of…
- **War**: troops needing a drug that could cure infections from injuries but also the illnesses that many of them got in a war that spread around the world.
- **Individual genius**: any of the men who were involved in the development of penicillin can be used as examples. Genius in medicine is about those people who see something and want to find out and develop it further, unlike the rest of us who would probably have done the washing up and done no more about it!

Make sure you can remember them all. Add them to your factor chart from page 12.

The big story about penicillin is how the first discovery was turned into a life-saving drug; and particularly evaluating the different roles of Florey, Chain and Fleming. The three men were jointly awarded a Nobel Prize for their achievements, but they were also rivals.

Make sure you are prepared for a 'Who was more important in the development of penicillin?' question by filling out this table. It will help you analyse:

- **what each person did** that was so marvellous
- **who you** think deserves the most credit.

NB it doesn't matter what your **conclusion** is, as long as it is based on evidence.

	Who?
Identified penicillin	
Proved that penicillin could cure infection in people	
Developed mass production of penicillin	
Got funding for the mass production of penicillin	
Developed a method to introduce penicillin into the body	
Carried out detailed experiments on penicillin to show that it could kill germs	
Used it as an antiseptic	
Used it as antibiotic	

Common question-type 5

- Are you surprised by…

When the Historical Source Investigation paper asks if you are surprised by a source, the examiner wants you to use your knowledge to put the sources in their historical **context**. Remember to:

- use your own knowledge and the other sources on the paper to judge whether a source **is typical** of the time or the topic
- express your own opinion, so your answer should say 'I am surprised because …' **or** 'I am **not** surprised because …'.
- look at both sides of the question – reasons why the source might be typical, and reasons why it might not be.

How to answer this question.

1. **Look closely** at Source A. What impression does it give you of Fleming?

2. **Read the caption**. What does that add to your understanding?

3. **Compare with other sources.** In this case you have only one but in an exam there will be several.

4. **Use your contextual knowledge**. What do you know about this topic and in particular about Fleming's reputation and whether it is deserved?

5. Then you are ready to **write your answer**. As always include **examples** from the sources that back up what you are saying.

NB This is a 9-mark question so allow up to 15 minutes.

Exam practice

1. Are you surprised by Source A? **[9]**

Source A: *Written by Howard Florey in a letter to the Medical Research Council in January 1944*

'My policy here has never been to interview the press nor allow them to get any information by telephone….

In contrast, Fleming has been interviewed without cease… with the result that he is put across as the discoverer of penicillin (which is true) with the implication that he did all the work leading to the discovery of its properties (which is not true).

Many of my colleagues feel things are going too far, and are getting unhappy at seeing so much of their own work going to glorify or even financially enrich someone else.'

Source B: *A stained glass window in St James Church, Paddington, made in 1952, showing Fleming in his laboratory. Fleming's laboratory was near to this church. This is a small part of a larger window that shows Jesus as saviour of the world.*

Answers online

Case study: The development of hospitals

1800: places to die

Today we think of hospitals as places to get well. In the early 1800s they were more likely to be places people died: from the disease they went in with, or a disease they got when they were there. Why were hospitals such unhealthy places?

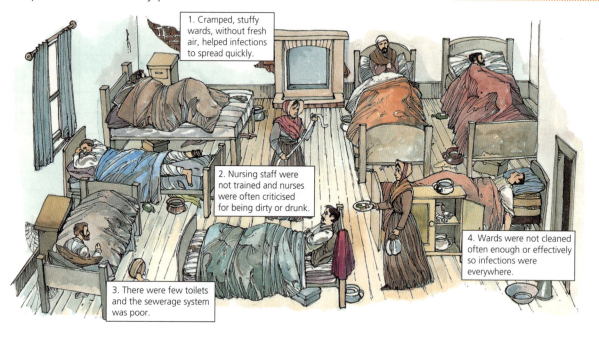

1. Cramped, stuffy wards, without fresh air, helped infections to spread quickly.

2. Nursing staff were not trained and nurses were often criticised for being dirty or drunk.

3. There were few toilets and the sewerage system was poor.

4. Wards were not cleaned often enough or effectively so infections were everywhere.

1900: Places to get well!

In the nineteenth century, hospitals were greatly improved particularly through the influence of **Florence Nightingale** who persuaded the government to change hospitals in Britain and to ensure nurses were properly trained.

- Nightingale believed that **sanitation** was the key and the first duty of her nurses was to keep everything clean.

- By 1900 infection and death rates in hospitals were much reduced and there were Nursing Schools all around the country teaching Nightingale's methods.

	Florence Nightingale (1820–1910)	**Mary Seacole (1805–1881)**
Background	From a rich English family who were opposed to her being a nurse. Father was active in the anti-slavery movement.	Born in Kingston, Jamaica. Father was a Scottish soldier and mother was a free black slave who ran a boarding house in Kingston.
Training	Despite her parents' opposition, she went to Germany to train as a nurse.	Her mother treated illness at her boarding house using herbal medicines. She passed this knowledge on to Mary.
Experience before 1854	Superintendent of a Woman's Hospital in London.	In 1850, cholera came to Kingston. She treated patients and saved many. Her fame grew.
How did she end up in Crimea?	*The Times* published articles about terrible conditions for soldiers in the Crimea and she volunteered to help. The government agreed (she had powerful friends including the Minister for War).	<ul><li>Heard about a cholera epidemic in the Crimea and travelled to London.</li><li>Volunteered to the army and to Nightingale but was turned down because of her lack of training.</li><li>Travelled to Crimea at her own expense.</li></ul>
What did she do in the Crimea?	<ul><li>Despite opposition from army doctors, she cleaned up the army hospital at Scutari some distance from the front.</li><li>Death rate in the army hospital dramatically reduced because diseases did not spread in these conditions.</li></ul>	<ul><li>Set up the British Hotel quite close to the front. She sold food and drink to the soldiers which paid for her to treat the soldiers.</li><li>Treated patients on the battlefield and is reported to have treated soldiers of both sides while the fighting was still going on.</li></ul>
What did she do when she returned?	<ul><li>She was a national heroine.</li><li>Began to work to improve the quality of nursing. Wrote *Notes on Nursing* and founded a School for Nurses at St Thomas' Hospital in London.</li><li>Awarded the Order of Merit in 1907.</li></ul>	<ul><li>She returned to London and went bankrupt as she had financed her trip herself.</li><li>*The Times* and *Punch* tried to support her but she never raised enough money to carry on treating patients.</li></ul>
Other attitudes or actions	<ul><li>She never accepted germ theory. She believed in miasma which was why she tried to clean hospitals, remove smells and improve ventilation.</li><li>She did not approve of women doctors.</li></ul>	<ul><li>She carried out operations on people suffering from knife and gunshot wounds.</li><li>During a cholera epidemic in Panama, she carried out an autopsy and was able to learn about the way the disease attacked the body.</li></ul>

Exam practice

1. How useful is Source A for finding out about Mary Seacole's contribution to improving hospitals in the 19th century? **[8]**

   Source A: *From a letter written by Florence Nightingale in 1870. Mary Seacole had asked for a reference as she was applying for a job nursing the troops in the Franco-Prussian War.*

   'I will not call it a bad house – but something like it. Anyone who employs Mrs Seacole will introduce much kindness – but also much drunkenness and improper conduct.'

Answers online

Examiner's tip

On page 47 you practised a usefulness question. You are going to practise that again. Refer back to the advice on page 47. See how you get on with this one.

The battle against infectious and non-infectious disease in the twentieth century

In the **twentieth century** infectious diseases were no longer the killers that they once were. The 'modern' killers were cancer and heart disease.

- **Lifestyle is seen as a major cause of disease**. Educating people to help them improve their lifestyle, such as explaining that stopping smoking helps to prevent cancer, can reduce the number of people getting cancer in the first place.

- **Early diagnosis can help prevent diseases developing further**. This happens through screening of people who are at risk, for example smear tests for cervical cancer for women over the age of 25, or screening for blood pressure levels.

- **Palliative care** is drugs/treatment for the symptoms of a disease rather than a cure, which allows people to live with the disease for many years, with a good quality of life (especially in the case of cancer).

However, **new infectious diseases** appeared in the twentieth century, for example **AIDS**, an epidemic in parts of Africa. There is no cure for AIDS, but drugs have been developed which lessen the symptoms and allow a good quality of life. However, these need to be cheaper and easier to obtain so that everyone who has AIDS can have them.

New so-called super-bugs have emerged that are resistant to antibiotics, such as MRSA. Until a cure can be found, cleaning hospital wards and washing hands with anti-bacterial lotion help to prevent MRSA. There are also old diseases that are still around and have become resistant to drugs, for example, malaria. Providing mosquito nets in affected areas helps to prevent the spread of malaria.

Exam practice

1. Briefly describe the career of Mary Seacole. [5]

2. 'The work of Fleming was the most important factor in the development of penicillin.' How far do you agree with this statement? Explain your answer. [8]

Answers online

KQ

Key question	Medicine in the nineteenth and twentieth centuries: fighting disease
What caused people to be healthy or unhealthy?	Infectious diseases such as smallpox; also blood poisoning
Who provided medical care?	– Quack doctors still existed – Doctors still expensive
What ideas did people have about the **causes** and **treatments** of illness and injuries?	**Causes:** miasma, spontaneous generation; **after 1860s: germ theory** **Treatments:** herbal treatments, vaccinations, magic bullets, penicillin, antibiotics
What caused diagnoses and treatments to remain the same or to change?	– Government, making vaccination compulsory – War helped support Pasteur and Koch – **Science and technology** (really important as it led to most developments in the fight against disease)
How far did new ideas and treatments affect the majority of the population?	– Germ theory – Vaccination against smallpox – Before 1948 drugs and antibiotics available to everyone at a cost

1.12 Surgery in the nineteenth and twentieth centuries

Before the nineteenth century, there were three main problems with carrying out surgery:

 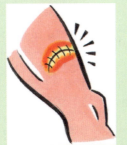 

Pain – patients could feel everything throughout the operation. They could die from the shock of the pain.

Infection – once operations were over, the wound often became infected and patients could die from this.

Blood loss – patients could bleed to death during and after the operation.

Operations were horrific, and were only carried out in an emergency. Because of the pain and the bleeding, a surgeon had to be **fast**, which led to mistakes such as cutting off the wrong part of the body. These problems were solved in the nineteenth and twentieth centuries.

Key content

- Case study: Developments in anaesthetics and antiseptics
- Developments in blood transfusion
- Modern surgery, transplanting organs and plastic surgery

Case study: Developments in anaesthetics and antiseptics

Revised ☐

Anaesthetics and the work of James Simpson

The problem of **pain** was the first to be solved in the 1840s with the development of **anaesthetics**. Different gases were used to send patients to sleep – the best of these was chloroform, which was discovered by James **Simpson** in 1847. He tried it first on himself before trying it out on patients.

Impact of anaesthetics

☺ When patients were asleep, they felt **no pain** which was good.

☺ As patients were still, and no longer dying from the shock of pain, **more complicated operations** could be done inside the body.

☹ Sometimes patients died from **too much chloroform**.

Revision task

Create a revision chart like this to sum up the key points about each development.

Problem	Pain
Solution	Anaesthetics
Key individual	
Key events (with dates)	
Limitations	
Opposition	

Examiner's tip

You might get asked questions about this case study in either the Development Study paper or the Source Investigation.

☹ The **death rate** from infection actually **went up** after the anaesthetics were developed, because: deeper operations meant **deeper infection**; more operations meant **more infection.** The full advantage of anaesthetics would not be seen until someone worked out how to prevent infection.

Opposition to anaesthetics

You should not be surprised by now that every development in medicine, however good it looks to us from our time, met with doubt, worry or outright opposition.

- Some doctors were against anaesthetics (especially during childbirth) because they thought pain was sent from God and should be endured.
- Others were alarmed at the deaths from chloroform itself and from infection as doctors tried more complex and longer operations.

However: anaesthetics got a big boost when Queen Victoria accepted chloroform to ease the pain of childbirth in 1857.

Antiseptics and the work of Joseph Lister

The problem of **infection** was solved by the development of **antiseptics**. Before germ theory was published in 1861, surgeons did not understand the causes of infection. So most reused bandages, wore dirty clothes and did not wash their hands.

Joseph **Lister** researched gangrene (decay of part of the body due to blood supply failure) and infection and knew all about the germ theory. In 1865 he started to use carbolic acid to kill germs during operations. It worked.

- **Before** he used carbolic spray nearly half of his amputations resulted in the death of the patient.
- **After** he used it only 15 per cent died.

He published his findings in 1867 and other surgeons began to use it.

Impact of antiseptics

☺ **Deaths** from infection after operations **fell**.

☹ **Not all doctors were as careful** as Lister was when using antiseptics, and so infections were still common.

Opposition to antiseptics

- Cleaning the wounds was hard work and slowed down operations. Many surgeons still prided themselves on speed.
- It seemed extreme. The carbolic spray soaked everything and everyone.
- Many people – surgeons included – still did not believe in germs. Surely something so small could not cause something so bad to happen? One surgeon regularly joked with his team to shut the door in case 'one of Mr Lister's microbes flies in'.

Key term

Carbolic acid – an organic compound originally extracted from coal tar to be used as an antiseptic

Common question-type 6

The final common question on the Historical Source Enquiry paper asks:

● Why was Source A published in ….?

As with all questions you need to study the content of the source carefully to understand its message and refer to other sources on the paper.

But for this kind of question the most important thing is your contextual knowledge. The question is about what attitudes people had at that time and how that explains the content or message of this source. So the more you know about the period, the easier this question will be.

Exam practice

1. Why was Source A published in the 1870s?   **[8]**

Source A: *'Operation Madness', published in the 1870s*

Source B: *Alexander Fleming recalling the time when he treated wounded soldiers in the First World War (1914–18)*

'I remember that I was told to make sure that I used antiseptics to dress wounds. So I used carbolic acid, boric acid and peroxide of hydrogen. I could see for myself that these antiseptics did not kill all microbes, but I was told the results were better than if no antiseptics had been used at all. At that time I was in no position to argue.'

Examiner's tip

How to answer this question.

1. Read the **question** carefully. Note the date: 1870s.

2. Study the **detail** in the source carefully. What is going on? Look in the foreground as well as the background.

3. Read the **caption**. The drawing has a title 'Operation Madness'. This is a clue to its message.

4. Work out the **message** of the source. What point is the artist making?

5. Use your **knowledge**. What was happening in surgery at this time?

6. **Cross-reference** to other sources on the paper. Here there is only one other but in the exam there will be 7–8.

7. Then you are ready to **write** an answer. As always include **examples** from the sources that back up what you are saying.

NB This is an 8-mark question so allow 12–15 minutes.

Answers online

Developments in blood transfusion

Revised

The final problem for surgery was **blood loss**. There had already been some developments prior to the nineteenth century:

- **Paré had begun using ligatures** to close arteries to stop bleeding. These were much more effective after antiseptics were developed.
- **Harvey had proved that there was only a certain amount of blood in the body**, which **needed to be replaced** if too much was lost.
- People first tried using animal blood to replace the human blood that was lost during operations – but this did not work!

Experiments to transfuse blood from other humans sometimes worked, but sometimes did not – no one understood why.

Then, in 1900 **Landsteiner** discovered **that** humans have **different blood groups**. These developments followed:

- In 1907 the first blood transfusion was done using matching blood groups.
- In the First World War, **methods of storing blood** were developed, so that blood could be taken **before** it was needed.
- During the Second World War, **national transfusion centres** were set up in the USA and Britain.

Key term

Ligature – a thread used to tie a blood vessel during an operation

Revision task

This is a really good time to make social networking profiles for Simpson, Lister and Landsteiner. There will be some overlap as they will have plenty of likes and friends in common, as well as needing each other's developments to improve surgery. See page 6 for guidance.

Modern surgery, transplanting organs and plastic surgery

Revised

X-rays

In 1895, **Röntgen** discovered **X-rays**. Doctors and surgeons could now see inside the body without having to cut it open!

Aseptic surgery

Antiseptic surgery (cleaning the wound) was replaced with **aseptic surgery** (cleaning everything in the room!).

Modern surgery

New developments in surgery in the twentieth and twenty-first centuries:

- **Keyhole surgery** can take place – this is cutting a tiny hole in the skin and using a fibre optic cable and cameras to see inside to perform delicate operations such as mending holes in the hearts of newborn babies.
- **Replacement surgery: joints can be replaced by plastic or metal ones** when the body's joints have worn out due to disease or age.
- **Transplant surgery:** The first heart transplant was carried out by Christiaan Barnard in 1967. In 1986 the first heart, liver and lung transplant was carried out. It is now possible to **transplant many vital organs from one body to another.**

Plastic surgery

- In the First World War, many soldiers suffered horrific burns. This led to the development of **skin grafts**, and for the first time doctors paid attention to the appearance of the patient after the operation.
- In the Second World War, the burned faces and hands of pilots were rebuilt, and surgeon Archie **McIndoe** used drugs such as penicillin to prevent any infection.
- The reconstruction of different parts of injured patients has been improved by skin grafts and the development of plastic skin. The first **facial transplant** was done in 2005 when a woman who had been facially disfigured from a dog attack was given the face tissue from a dead person's face.

Revision task

Modern surgery is a particularly good topic for illustrating the influence of science and technology on medicine. Add the following examples to your factor chart:

- development of x-rays
- computers and cameras allowing keyhole surgery
- improvements in plastic and metals allowing replacement of body parts.

Improvements in surgery raise ethical issues. Hi-tech surgery is very **expensive** and there is only a limited amount of funding for healthcare.

- Should we prioritise some operations over others?
- Should someone have a heart transplant which would cost the same as about fifty hip transplants?
- Should a shy teenager have their nose made smaller so that they gain confidence?

Exam practice

1. Explain how war has led to changes in medicine. **[7]**

2. Explain how the problem of bleeding during surgery was overcome. **[7]**

3. 'Simpson is more important than Lister in the history of medicine.' How far do you agree with this statement? Explain your answer. **[8]**

Answers online

Key question	Medicine in the nineteenth and twentieth centuries: surgery
What ideas did people have about the causes and treatments of illness and injuries?	Germ theory
What caused treatments to remain the same or to change?	– Anaesthetics (chloroform) – Antiseptics (carbolic spray) – Blood groups – blood transfusions
How far did new ideas and treatments affect the majority of the population?	Transplants, keyhole surgery

1.13 Public health in the nineteenth and twentieth centuries

Public health means what governments do about the health of ordinary people.

- In the nineteenth century this was focused on **cleaning up towns**.
- In the twentieth century it was focused on providing **welfare and healthcare for poor people**.

> ## Key content
>
> - The impact of industrialisation on living conditions and on health and hygiene in the nineteenth and twentieth centuries
> - Case study: The development of public health systems in the nineteenth century
> - The reforms of the Liberal governments, 1906–1914
> - The introduction and impact of the National Health Service
> - The continuing debate about the provision of healthcare

The impact of industrialisation on living conditions and on health and hygiene in the nineteenth and twentieth centuries

Revised ☐

Britain was going through an industrial revolution in the nineteenth century. Lots of people moved from villages to towns to find work in factories.

- They had to live close to their places of work so many **low quality houses** were quickly built.
- **Smoke** from the coal-fired factories filled the air.
- Houses were close together. They did not have **running water** or **toilets**.
- **Diseases** spread quickly in the overcrowded **slums**, particularly the deadly disease cholera. There were cholera epidemics in London in the 1830s, 1840s and 1850s.
- Due to the poor conditions **life expectancy** was much lower in the towns than it was in the countryside.

> **Revision task**
>
> Draw your own annotated sketch to show the dangers to health caused by rapid industrialisation.

Government response

To start with, the government did nothing about living conditions in the slums for two main reasons.

- In 1820, **only rich men were allowed to vote**, and they had good living conditions. The poor people who lived in these slums could not vote.
- The common attitude was *laissez-faire*, i.e. 'don't get involved'. Governments at that time believed ordinary people should be free to run their lives and that poor people should help themselves. It was not the role of government to solve social problems.

Case study: The development of public health systems in the nineteenth century

1832	Cholera epidemic in British towns. This kills both the rich and the poor.
1842	**Edwin Chadwick** publishes his *Report into the Sanitary Conditions of the Labouring Population of Great Britain.* He writes that poor people are living in dirty conditions which causes a huge amount of illness, so people are too sick to work. He suggests that by improving drainage and sewers, removing waste from streets, providing clean water supplies and appointing medical officers, fewer workers would fall ill and need time off work.
1848	Chadwick's recommendations lead to the first **Public Health Act**. Towns are told to clean up, **but there is no punishment from the government if they do not**. There is opposition as people don't want to pay taxes for improvements to the towns, especially the rich people who are living quite well and have a *laissez-faire* attitude to the poor. Some people don't like the interference of the government.
1849	Another outbreak of **cholera** – 10,000 people die in three months in London.
1849	**John Snow** publishes *On the Mode of Communication of Cholera.* He **proves that cholera is spread through water**, not bad air.
1853	**Compulsory vaccination** against smallpox.
1854	John Snow continues to publish proof that **cholera is spread through water**. Clean water is essential to prevent cholera.
1858	The **Great Stink** in London – the summer is very hot and the smell from the River Thames grows worse and worse; the worst smells are at the Houses of Parliament!
1861	Pasteur publishes his **germ theory**, proving bacteria cause disease.
1866	Law saying that towns must have a **clean water** and **sewage supply** as soon as possible. **Inspectors** will check!
1867	Poor, working men get **the vote**, so looking after poor people becomes a vote winner.
1875	**Public Health Act:** Towns **must** keep streets clean and sewers **must** be cleaned. Towns can charge taxes to do this.

The big difference between 1848 and 1875

The **1848 Act** was voluntary – towns did not have to clean up. Some did. Some didn't. The **1875 Act** was compulsory – towns had to do it whether they wanted to or not.

Why did the government decide to make it compulsory in 1875? Three big reasons:

- **Rich people** died of cholera so politicians took it seriously.
- **Poor people** got the vote in 1867, so looking after poor people became a vote winner.
- **The germ theory** proved there was a point to cleaning away dirt.

Examiner's tip

You might get asked questions about this case study in either the Development Study paper or the Source Investigation.

Revision task

Many factors lead to the Public Health Act of 1875. From pages 65–66 pick out examples of these factors and, using the colours below, add them to your factor chart.

- Science and technology
- Individual genius
- Government and political reform

Examiner's tip

Make sure you remember these three reasons and expand on them in your examination answers.

John Snow, cholera and a water pump

- John Snow did not believe in miasma. His theory was that cholera was transmitted through infected water. Remember he did not know about germs. Pasteur had not done his work yet.

- During the 1854 cholera epidemic in London Snow mapped the deaths in a small area of London and found that those who died shared one water pump.

- He removed the handle of the pump. Deaths went down. Simple as that but what a breakthrough!

Examiner's tip

Sources about public health

There is a massive range of sources about public health. It was a major preoccupation in the nineteenth century with government reports and debates; newspaper articles and cartoons; jokes; letters; maps. However, a common angle for Source Investigation is the role of specific individuals or events in this development, for example: the role of Edwin Chadwick in alerting people to the true living conditions of poor people; the role of John Snow in helping people understand that cholera came from infected water; or the role of 'The Great Stink' in forcing Parliament to take public health seriously.

Exam practice

1. Why was Source A published in the 1850s? **[8]**

Source A: *Published by* Punch *magazine in the 1850s*

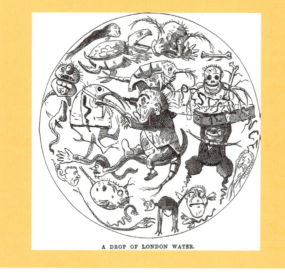

A DROP OF LONDON WATER.

Source B: *John Snow, who proved that cholera was in the water, writing in 1854*

'On proceeding to the spot, I found that nearly all the deaths had taken place within a short distance of the [Broad Street] pump. There were only ten deaths in houses situated decidedly nearer to another street-pump. In five of these cases the families of the deceased persons informed me that they always sent to the pump in Broad Street, as they preferred the water to that of the pumps which were nearer. In three other cases, the deceased were children who went to school near the pump in Broad Street ...'

Answers online

Examiner's tip

You have already met this kind of question. Remember the advice on page 61.

1. Read the **question** carefully. Note the date: 1850s.

2. Use your **knowledge**. What was happening at this time?

3. Read the **caption**. What does 'A Drop of London Water' mean? This is a clue to its message.

4. Study the **detail** in the source carefully. What does it show?

5. Work out the **message** of the source. What point is the artist making?

6. **Cross-reference** with the other sources – here there is only one other but in the exam there will be several.

7. Then you are ready to **write** an answer. As always include **examples** from the sources that back up what you are saying.

NB This is an 8-mark question so allow 12–15 minutes

Examiner's tip

Two things you should be doing with sources all the time:

- cross-referencing
- evaluating reliability.

Even when a question does not directly ask you to cross-reference or evaluate reliability you still need to do so, because they are basic steps in using sources. You always need to compare a source with other sources and decide whether you trust what a source is saying.

The reforms of the Liberal governments, 1906–1914

In 1906, a new Liberal government was elected and took measures to improve everyday life.

	Reforms and how they helped the poor	Limitations of the reforms
1906	**Free school meals** provided for children in need.	This was not compulsory so many councils ignored the system and not all children in need got them.
	Workers Compensation Act – workers got compensation for any injuries they got at work.	
1907	**School medical inspections** – nurses or doctors had to carry out medical checks on children in schools.	
1908	**Children's Charter** • Punishments were given to those neglecting or treating children cruelly. • Children were sent to borstals rather than adult prisons.	
	Pensions were introduced for those over the age of 70.	Pensions were refused to people who had not worked.
	Maximum of **eight-hour day** for miners.	
1909	**Labour exchanges** were set up to help unemployed people find work.	Some of the jobs were temporary; the government did not create new jobs.
1910	**Half-day off** a week for shop workers.	
1911	**National Insurance Act** • **Free medical treatment and sick pay** if workers were ill in return for a payment of 4d a week. • **Unemployment pay** (dole) for 15 weeks in return for a payment of 2½d a week.	Medical treatment was only for the wage earner, not for his family. Payments were high for poor people and the benefits were not enough for a family to live off. They also stopped after a number of weeks.
	MPs were paid. This gave working men the opportunity to stand for election.	

Why were the reforms passed?

- Studies of towns like York by **researchers like Rowntree** showed that too many people still lived in poverty.
- **The Boer War** had underlined this point as two-thirds of men who volunteered to fight were not fit enough to do so.
- **Trade Unions** and the **Labour Party**, which supported workers, were gaining power; the Liberal party needed to get their votes.
- **Lloyd George and other MPs** genuinely wanted to do something to improve the lives of poor people in Britain – politicians *can* have good motives, you know!

> **Revision task**
>
> Record one example (with dates) of how the Liberal reforms helped each of the following groups:
>
> - the unemployed
> - the elderly
> - school-age children
> - shop workers
> - miners.

The introduction and impact of the National Health Service

In 1942, **William Beveridge** was asked by the government to report on the state of Britain. He wrote a report which called for a **welfare state**, to end the 'Five Giants/Evils' that made people poor:

| Disease | Want | Ignorance | Idleness | Squalor |

The welfare state would provide **free education, free healthcare, unemployment benefits** and **pensions**. To fund this, Beveridge called for everyone to pay a **National Insurance** contribution out of their wages.

When the Labour party won the election in 1945, they immediately began to create the welfare state.

One of its major features was the **National Health Service (NHS)**. This aspect of the welfare state is most important in the history of medicine. The NHS was established in 1948. Under the NHS, **all medical treatment was free** and doctors were paid by the government.

Some doctors **opposed** the NHS because they thought they would lose money from the patients who were currently paying money to them for private services. **Aneurin Bevan**, the Minister for Health, promised to pay doctors a salary and he allowed them to continue to have fee-paying private patients as well as working for the NHS.

Revision task

Draw around your hand then label your 'hand map' with the key facts about the introduction of the National Health Service

Revision task

Annotate this source to explain the meaning of each feature.

DOTHEBOYS HALL
"It still tastes awful."

⬆ **A cartoon published in 1948. It shows Aneurin Bevan giving doctors medicine they don't like.**

The continuing debate about the provision of healthcare

Issues with the provision of healthcare

- Free healthcare is popular, waiting lists are growing, and it is hard to get emergency appointments with GPs.

- It is becoming harder and harder in some areas to find a National Health dentist, as they get more money from private patients.

- The NHS needs more and more money each year to ensure that it can provide free healthcare for all. However, not all healthcare is free. Adults pay: for prescriptions; to visit the dentist; and for eye tests.

- So, choices have to be made. The NHS has a finite budget, so there is a debate over whether conditions like infertility should be treated on the NHS, or whether the budget should be prioritised for people who are ill. Should people who make themselves ill by smoking, or by being obese, be allowed to get free treatment?

- The media talk about a 'postcode lottery', as it depends on your local NHS area whether or not you can get certain treatments for many different conditions, including cancer.

Exam practice

1. Describe how industrialisation affected the health of people in Britain. **[5]**

2. Explain why the Liberal government of 1906 introduced measures to help the poor. **[7]**

3. 'The main reason why public health was improved in the nineteenth century was because the working classes got the vote.' How far do you agree with this statement? Explain your answer. **[8]**

Answers online

KQ

Key question	Medicine in the nineteenth and twentieth centuries: public health
What caused people to be healthy or unhealthy?	– Living conditions – Poverty
Who provided medical care?	Public Health Act, 1848
What ideas did people have about the causes and treatments of illness and injuries?	Germ theory
What caused diagnoses and treatments to remain the same or to change?	– Germ theory – Individuals, e.g. Pasteur, Snow
How far did new ideas and treatments affect the majority of the population?	– In the nineteenth century, only the wealthy had homes with toilets and piped water; the majority of people shared outside toilets and got their water from a street pump – In the twentieth century, everyone received fresh water and all new houses had their own toilets – Public Health Act – taxes

2 The American West, 1840–1895

2.1 How did the Plains Indians live on the Great Plains?

Focus points

- Why did many white Americans at first regard the Great Plains as the 'Great American Desert'?
- How were the **Plains Indians** able to live on the Great Plains?
- What were the beliefs of the Plains Indians?
- Did all Plains Indians have the same beliefs and the same way of life?

Why did many white Americans at first regard the Great Plains as the 'Great American Desert'?

Revised ☐

The Great Plains were in the middle of North America, stretching from the Mississippi river in the east to the Rocky mountains in the west, and from Canada in the north to Mexico in the south.

- **Summers** were hot and dry, reaching up to 40°C.
- **Winters** were cold and snowy, well below 0°C.
- There was **very little water**.
- There was lots of **strong wind** all year round.
- Vegetation was **grassland**: long prairie grass in the east, shorter near the Rockies.

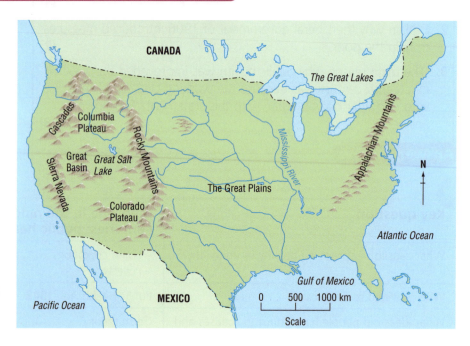

White Europeans first settled in the far east of North America. **The climate there was similar to the climate in Europe**.

The **natural obstacles** of the Appalachian Mountains and the Mississippi River made it **difficult for them to explore** further west. But, when they did, they found such harsh conditions that they believed that no one could settle there, and it became known as the Great American Desert.

To answer questions about the American West it is vital you understand and remember its geography. Without looking at the map on page 70, try to label the five numbered features here.

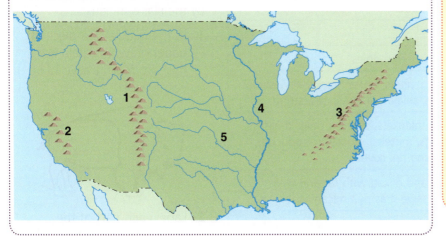

How were the Plains Indians able to live on the Great Plains?

Revised

The white Americans may have thought the Plains were a desert but the Plains Indians had lived there for thousands of years. They had adapted their way of life to the harsh climate and environment. In order to survive, they were **nomadic hunter-gatherers.**

Key terms

Nomad/Nomadic – people who do not live in one place but travel from place to place

Hunter-gatherers – people who get their food by hunting and by gathering what grows naturally (rather than by farming)

BUFFALO: The main source of food for the Plains Indians was the buffalo. In the early nineteenth century, there were millions of buffalo roaming on the Plains. The buffalo supplied many of the Indians' needs.

HORSES: The Plains Indians first hunted on foot **but, in 1640, Spanish invaders brought the first horses to North America**. They did not give these horses to the Indians, but the **Indians captured many of them** and bred and traded them between their tribes. Indians then started to use horses to hunt buffalo. **They valued their horses highly** – a Plains Indian was rich if he had lots of horses, and warfare between tribes was mainly because of horse stealing.

THE PRACTICE OF EXPOSURE: If a member of the tribe was moving too slowly due to illness or old age, then they could choose to allow the majority of the tribe to carry on and to **remain behind on the Plains to die from exposure**.

Uses of the buffalo

When a buffalo was killed, the women of the tribe would prepare all the different parts of the buffalo to use in a variety of ways.

Buffalo part	How it was used
Horns	Cups
Skull	Used in religious ceremonies
Rawhide (skin before being prepared)	Bags, belts, containers, horse harnesses, lashings, masks, sheaths, shields, snow-shoes, string
Tanned hide (leather)	Bags, bedding, blankets, clothes, dolls, dresses, drums, leggings, mittens, moccasins, pouches, robes, saddle and tipi covers
Flesh	Cooked, dried and mixed with fat and wild cherries to preserve it as pemmican
Dung	Fuel (buffalo chips) and smoked by men in special ceremonies
Bladder	Food bags
Fat	Cooking, soap, hair grease
Bones	Arrowheads, knives, tools
Heart	Cut from the body and left on the ground to give new life to the herd. To the Plains Indians the buffalo was sacred – man's relative who gave his life so people could live. The heart might also be eaten raw so that the warrior could take the strength of the buffalo.
Tongue	Used as a hairbrush or eaten raw as a delicacy

ORGANISATION: Each tribe had to be well organised to live on the Plains. Each tribe had a **chief** who had power because of their **wisdom**, their **spiritual power** or their **skills as hunters and warriors**. There were **no formal laws**, and if a brave (warrior) did not want to follow the orders of the chief he did not have to. Decisions were reached by the **council** of the tribe, who would keep talking until everyone agreed. Important decisions had to be agreed by all the men in a tribe. **A pipe would be smoked** during the discussions to make sure that the spirit world would know what they were saying and help them make good decisions. Some of the men in the tribe belonged to a **warrior society** such as the Dog Soldiers of the Cheyenne. They were skilled in fighting and would help the chief and elders in their war planning.

Revision task

Draw a diagram to help you remember how the different parts of the buffalo were used by the Plains Indians.

1. In the middle of a piece of paper draw a buffalo like this – it doesn't have to be very good!

2. Label each part of the buffalo shown in the table – insides *and* outsides.

3. Next to each label, write **how** the Plains Indians used that part. Use four colours to show if it was used for clothing, religion, the home or weapons.

Key terms

Chief – leader of each tribe; there were many different sorts of chiefs, for example a war chief, a peace chief

Council – group of elders or experts of a tribe, who would meet to discuss any decisions that needed to be made about the group

Warrior societies – groups of braves who would support the tribe during war

HOMES: The Plains Indians needed to **move around the Plains** so that they could follow the herds of buffalo. They did this by living in **tipis** which could be put up and taken down in about ten minutes. A tipi was **made of buffalo skin** supported by wood poles to form a tent. The buffalo skin was highly decorated. When it was time to move, the women would use the poles to make a sled and the contents of the tipi were wrapped up in the buffalo skin and attached to the poles. This was called a **travois**, and was then pulled by horses, dogs or people.

FAMILY LIFE: Plains Indians travelled together in family groups called tribes. These were made up of between 10 and 50 families. The men did the hunting, and protected the tribe. **Men often died young through hunting and warfare** so there were more women than men in the tribe. Because of this, a rich man (a good hunter) could have more than one wife (because he would need them to prepare the number of buffalo he caught). The women looked after the tipi, prepared food and made clothing and other items. Children learned the skills they needed for their adult life.

INDIAN WARFARE: Warfare was very important to the Plains Indians. The most common reason for war between tribes and nations was **because of horses**. An Indian warrior was judged by the number of horses that he owned, so tribes raided others to steal horses and then were raided in turn in revenge. Horses were a bit like money to the Plains Indians – if you had lots of horses you were rich! If your horses were stolen, you were no longer 'rich', or important, and so you were humiliated as well.

It was rare for the Plains Indians to **fight to the death** because men were so valuable in the buffalo hunt. Instead, they **counted coup.** This involved the warrior touching his enemy with a coup stick. It was considered brave and meant that a warrior was skilful enough to get close to his enemy but did not value him enough to kill him. Indian battle dress often showed how many times the warrior had counted coup. Plains Indian battles were short, often involving quick raids, and a brave Indian lived to fight another day.

Plains Indians used tomahawks and bows and arrows in their hunting and warfare. If they killed anyone they would **scalp** them. They believed that if a warrior had lost his scalp, he could not go into the afterlife whole and be able to do well there. Alternatively they would cut his ankle or wrist tendons, which meant that the warrior would not be able to run or fire arrows when he reached the **Happy Hunting Ground**.

Key terms

Tipi/Tepee – tent made of buffalo skin which the Plains Indians lived in

Travois – method of transporting the tipi and contents by using the poles to drag along the wrapped contents

Tribe – a small group of Plains Indians made up of several families. Can also be called a 'band'. There were many tribes in a nation

Key terms

Counting coup – touching the enemy without killing him, an Indian idea of bravery

Scalping – ensuring that your enemy could not go into the Happy Hunting Ground by removing his scalp, hair and skin

Happy Hunting Ground – where Plains Indians believed they would go after they died

Revision task

Many white Americans considered the Plains Indians to be cowards and savages. Why do you think they felt like this?

For each of these customs

- counting coup
- scalping
- exposure
- polygamy

write a brief description of

- what it was
- why the Plains Indians did it
- what the white Americans would think of it.

What were the beliefs of the Plains Indians?

LAND: They believed that land was sacred and could not be bought or sold – it belonged to everyone. Selling it would be like someone trying to sell you the wind or the air.

THE SPIRIT WORLD: One of the major tribes, the **Lakota** Sioux, believed in Waken Tanka – a great spirit who had created the world and controlled all of nature. They believed that **spirits lived in all living things**, and that the **spirits could influence their lives**.

CIRCLES: They saw life as a circle from birth to death. The sun was a circle; the moon was a circle. Their tipis would be circular. They would put their camps in a circle to remain close to the spirits.

DANCES AND CEREMONIES: They believed that they could get closer to the spirits by ceremonies knowns as dances. This was not dancing as we know it, but **meditation, fasting or enduring pain.** The most famous was the **Sun Dance**. This involved fasting and contemplation followed by suspending warriors from the roof by putting skewers through holes in their pectoral (chest) muscles. **Dances would take place before battles or raids, and before and after a buffalo hunt, to get close to the spirits who would help them.**

VISIONS: When young men reached adolescence, they would fast and sit in a sweat lodge in order to get a vision. The medicine man or shaman of the tribe would interpret this vision into what the future held for him, and through this they would provide him with his adult name, for example 'Crazy Horse'. Visions were also important in later life. Sitting Bull removed strips of skin from his body before the Battle of Little Bighorn, which gave him a vision. The vision was of men in blue uniforms falling, and was a factor in the unshakeable belief of the Plains Indians that they would win the battle (see page 97).

AFTERLIFE: When they died, Plains Indians believed that they would go to the Happy Hunting Ground where they would meet everyone they knew during their life. There was no belief in a heaven or a hell.

Key terms

Waken Tanka – Great Spirit who controlled all of nature

Sweat lodge – a method of gaining visions for younger men; it involved fasting and spending time in the lodge which would be sealed and contain burning herbs to cause visions

Vision – the way in which Plains Indians men contacted the spirits

Medicine man – the member of the tribe who could contact and interpret contact with the spirits

Revision task

Create your own revision cards about Plains Indian beliefs from what you have read here and what you can remember from your history lessons. On one side write the belief, on the other write the facts.

- Give yourself five points for each fact you write down.
- Give yourself five extra points for any fact you can represent in the form of a picture or diagram.
- Try to get 50 points in total.

Examiner's tip

A lot of the history of the American West was written by the white Americans who had negative attitudes to the Plains Indians. But a good historian will try to be **objective** and to understand the Plains Indians' beliefs and customs in their own right rather than as the white Americans saw them.

For your exam you need to show that you know

- **how** the Plains Indians lived
- **why** they lived that way, even if it seemed completely alien to the white Americans with whom they came into contact.

Did all Plains Indians have the same beliefs and the same way of life?

Revised

There were **many different nations** that were known as Plains Indians. Each had its own traditions, customs and characteristics. For example:

The Sioux: the largest and best-known Plains Indian nation. In 1840 they were the **most important nation** in the central Plains as they had lived and hunted the buffalo there for a very long time.

The Sioux were divided into Dakota, Lakota and Nakota. Each spoke a different version of the same dialect.

The Cheyenne: also based in the centre of the Plains. Traditionally they were allies of the Sioux and were considered to be **more peaceful** than other tribes.

The Cherokee: had once been **farmers** but had been moved off their farming land in the East after 1840 and had become Plains Indians.

The Crow: traditionally the **enemies of the Sioux**.

The Comanche: based in the South Plains and considered **very skilled horsemen**.

Oral tradition: the Plains Indians did not write down their traditions and customs, or their history. Instead, they passed down stories orally from generation to generation. Because of the deaths of so many Plains Indians during the nineteenth century, it is difficult to be exact about the specific beliefs and ways of life of each nation.

Nations would meet together in the summer. Some nations were traditional allies and others were enemies. This did not help in their uniting when it came to fighting the white Europeans: most of the time, the nations were split across the Plains or fighting each other. This situation had changed by the 1870s when all Indian nations did unite against the whites.

Revision task

Choose two examples of differences between tribes and two examples of similarities. They could be useful for your exam.

Exam practice

1. Briefly describe the way of life of the Plains Indians. **[5]**

2. Explain how the Plains Indians were able to live on the Great Plains. **[7]**

3. 'The Plains Indians were savages.' Why did white Americans come to this conclusion? **[8]**

Answers online

Examiner's tip

See advice on answering exam questions on pages 5–9.

2.2 Why did people travel to the West? The pioneers and the Mormons

Until the 1840s, white European settlement was almost all on the east coast of North America. It was very difficult to explore or travel across the continent and people did not believe it was possible to live in the Great American Desert. Over the next 45 years, a **massive change** happened and **by 1890 people from the East had settled all over North America**. The first wave consisted of hunters known as **mountain men**, people heading for the west coast, known as **pioneers**, and the Mormons.

Focus points

- What were the experiences of the first pioneer families in the 1840s when they travelled west?
- Why did the Mormons go west?
- How were the Mormons able to survive the journey and be successful in Salt Lake Valley?

What were the experiences of the first pioneer families in the 1840s when they travelled west?

Revised ☐

The first pioneer families travelled west in the 1840s, to settle as farmers on the west coast in the states of California and Oregon. Why did they move?

Pull factors (what was good about the West)	Push factors (what was bad about the East)
People listened to the stories of the **mountain men who described the West as a place of opportunity**, where the sun always shone, the rivers were full of fish and the land was perfect for farming.	In 1837 the USA was hit by an **economic depression**. Banks collapsed, people lost their savings, wages were cut, people became unemployed.
From 1842, the government offered free land to anyone who would settle on the west coast.	Problems in Europe led more Europeans to move to the USA. So land in the East **was overcrowded and expensive**.

However, to reach the west coast of North America meant travelling across the Great Plains and the Rocky Mountains. The journey to California and Oregon was a long one. It was over 3800 km (about 2300 miles) and took at least 6 months by horse-drawn wagon.

Pioneers travelling to the West met in one of the towns by the Missouri River to stock up and prepare for the journey. They would join up into groups to travel together for safety.

They travelled in a wagon in which they had to take everything that they needed on the journey, and also what they needed for their new life in the West. This included **livestock**, and seeds to plant. They bought these things in the towns on the Missouri River where prices were often really high.

They would then travel along one of the trails that other groups had used before (see map). Many groups took a mountain man as guide.

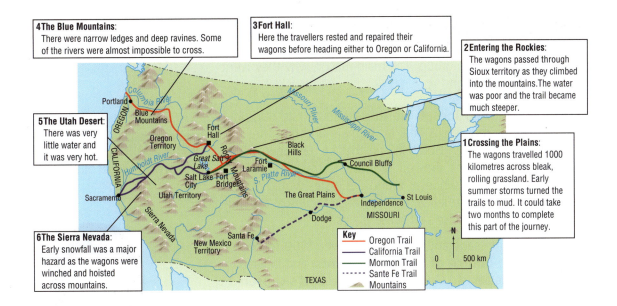

4 The Blue Mountains: There were narrow ledges and deep ravines. Some of the rivers were almost impossible to cross.

3 Fort Hall: Here the travellers rested and repaired their wagons before heading either to Oregon or California.

2 Entering the Rockies: The wagons passed through Sioux territory as they climbed into the mountains. The water was poor and the trail became much steeper.

5 The Utah Desert: There was very little water and it was very hot.

1 Crossing the Plains: The wagons travelled 1000 kilometres across bleak, rolling grassland. Early summer storms turned the trails to mud. It could take two months to complete this part of the journey.

6 The Sierra Nevada: Early snowfall was a major hazard as the wagons were winched and hoisted across mountains.

Key
Oregon Trail
California Trail
Mormon Trail
Sante Fe Trail
Mountains

Different pioneers faced different experiences but there were many dangers and problems that they all shared.

The geography was harsh

- Travellers had to cross the Missouri and the Platte Rivers.
- They had to climb **up** into the Rocky Mountains, often using **pulley and ropes** to winch up the wagons. Little water available.
- They had to climb **down** into the desert lands where the temperatures could reach 38°C and there was **no water**.

The weather conditions were dangerous

- Travellers left the Missouri in April so that they could cross the Rockies before the winter **snow storms** set in.
- That meant they crossed the Great Plains at the **hottest** time. With little water there, people could die from **dehydration**.
- The heat could also cause extreme and dangerous **storms**.
- When they reached the Rocky Mountains, they had to go on: they did not have enough resources to cross the Plains again.
- If they were caught in the mountains in winter, the consequences could be terrible. The **Donner Party**, for example, tried to take a short cut but got trapped in the Sierra Mountains. It started to snow; they ran out of food. Some of these party left to get help but some of these died of starvation on the way and the others had to resort to eating the dead to survive. When they reached help, a rescue party went back to the original group – half were dead and the others were partly mad.

There were attacks from animals and other humans

- **Bears and mountain lions** could attack the wagons for food.
- **Plains Indians** often helped the pioneers, by trading goods or being guides, but occasionally they did attack them to take horses or hostages.

Food was scarce

- The pioneers took as much food as they could for the journey, but had to keep enough to survive once in the West.
- Sometimes the livestock for their farms could not keep going so they killed the animals and dried the meat.

Revision task

Create a detailed memory map.

1. In the centre, write 'The dangers that the pioneers faced when they travelled west'. Then draw branches from the centre for each problem: **Geography, Weather, Attacks, Food**.

2. Add key words, phrases and doodles to help you remember the details, such as a mountain bear or a snowflake.

Examiner's tip

Students often wonder why there was not more conflict between the early pioneers and the Plains Indians. This was because the pioneers were simply passing through. They did not pose a threat to the Plains Indians' way of life because **they did not want to settle on the Plains**.

Why did the Mormons go west?

The Mormons were a religions group. The main reason why they went west was to escape persecution.

In 1823, a poor farmer called **Joseph Smith** claimed he had dug up some gold plates on the mountains near his home – and that these plates contained messages from God. He said that he had been visited by an angel called **Moroni** who showed him how to translate what the plates said. They said that whoever found the plates would restore the Church of Jesus Christ in America, and be ready for Jesus' second coming – to America. No one else saw these plates.

- Smith preached his message and by 1830 had over 1000 followers. They were called the **Church of Latter-day Saints**, and believed that if they were obedient to God they would be **God's chosen people**.
- The **Mormons called non-Mormons Gentiles**. Mormons firmly believed that Gentiles were **godless** and they told people who believed themselves to be good Christian people that they would not go to heaven. Smith's success frightened non-Mormons.

Kirtland (1831–37)

- Smith moved to **Ohio**, to a village called Kirtland which was his **Zion** (Heavenly City) in the 1830s. He built a temple and a bank. In 1837, the bank collapsed in the financial crisis of that year. Both Mormon and non-Mormon investors lost their money. This made the Mormons even more unpopular!

Missouri (1837–38)

- The Mormons then moved to Independence, Missouri.
- The Mormons were friendly towards the Indians, and also wanted to end slavery, which was widespread in the USA.
- They formed a secret organisation called the **Danites**, which many non-Mormons believed had been set up to attack them.
- The governor of Missouri wanted to drive out the Mormons. He even went so far as to say that the Mormons should be exterminated.

Nauvoo (1839–46)

- The Mormons fled to Illinois and moved into a town called Commerce, which they renamed **Nauvoo**.
- By 1845, 11,000 Mormons lived in Nauvoo. There were so many Mormons that the two political parties in Illinois wanted their support. The Mormons were allowed to have their own laws and a private army in return for their votes. However non-Mormons in Illinois were afraid of this increasing political power of the Mormons.

> **Key terms**
>
> **Moroni** – angel of god who appeared to Smith

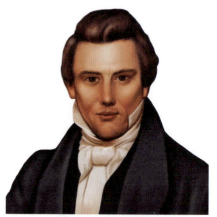

↑ Joseph Smith

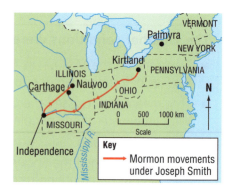

> **Key terms**
>
> **Danites** – secret army/police formed by the Mormons
>
> **Nauvoo** – city formed by the Mormons whose name means 'beautiful plantation'

Joseph Smith is killed

- Smith announced that he had received a revelation from God which said that some Mormons could have **more than one wife** (polygamy).
- Smith was also planning to run for **President of the USA**.
- Non-Mormons were outraged. Mobs started roaming the countryside trying to kill Mormons. A mob killed Smith in June 1845.

Brigham Young moves the Mormons west ✐

The Mormons were now unpopular wherever they tried to settle, but they wanted to stay together and live according to their own beliefs. A new leader emerged: **Brigham Young**. Young realised that the Mormons needed to move to **a place that no one else wanted** in order to build their Mormon society. In September 1845, Young made the decision to move the Mormons to Salt Lake Valley, an area in the middle of the Rockies. The land there was poor and dry.

Revision task

The Mormons moved west because they were unpopular with non-Mormons.
Make a table to explain why each belief or event made them unpopular.

Belief/Event	
Their beliefs about Moroni	
Their beliefs about non-Mormons	
Financial crisis of 1837	
Their success in attracting converts	
Polygamy	

Examiner's tip

In answering this question, remember that non-Mormons were **more afraid of what the Mormons could become than what the Mormons believed**. For example, take the Mormon practice of polygamy. The majority of settlers in the USA were Christians, who believed a man should have only one wife. They disapproved of polygamy. But equally important they feared it because polygamy would mean that the Mormons would produce many more children and therefore there would be lots more Mormons in the future.

↑ **Brigham Young**

Exam practice

1. What can you learn from Source A about attitudes to the Mormons in the 1840s?   [5]

Source A: *A cartoon from the 1840s commenting on polygamy, titled, 'The Elders' Happy Home'*

Answers online

How were the Mormons able to survive the journey and be successful in Salt Lake Valley?

❮ How did they survive the journey west?

In early 1846, Brigham Young moved 1500 Mormons – men, women and children – 2250 km to the Great Salt Lake.

↑ **Map showing the Mormon route to Salt Lake Valley**

- The Mormons were used to working together, and they were united in their common belief.
- They travelled in stages. Supplies were taken in advance and left at different points along the route so that people following on could use them instead of having to carry large amounts of supplies with them.
- The journey was planned and guided carefully, and plenty of time was allowed to make sure that everyone arrived before the first snow fell.
- There were problems during the journey but everyone helped each other to solve them.

↗ Making a success of Salt Lake Valley

Salt Lake was not a fertile area for farming. There were few raw materials, such as iron. So it was difficult for the Mormons to be **self-sufficient**. However, by 1847, its population was 1500 and more and more settlements were being established. How did they succeed?

- Young decided that no one could own the land or pure water.
- Each person was given a plot of land to grow their own food (see plan).
- **Skilled workers** were carefully identified and given relevant jobs.
- Church leaders controlled the farming and what was built.
- Water was essential. The Mormons worked together to build a main irrigation ditch through the farming land. Side ditches were then dug so that all the land could be irrigated. Each person was given an exact time when they were allowed to draw water from the main ditch.

> **Key term**
>
> **Self-sufficient** – not relying on anyone else, which means growing and making everything that you need, including growing cotton, shearing sheep for clothes, and making your own tools from iron

Salt Lake City

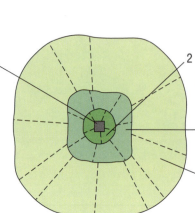

1 The Temple and the Temple Square were in the centre of the city.

Around the square, wide streets marked off blocks of land. These were each divided into plots for houses and gardens. Each family was given a plot.

2 The inner area provided five-acre plots for the young skilled workers and mechanics who had little time to work on the land.

3 The middle area provided ten-acre plots for those with small families or elderly couples whose children had left home.

4 The outer area provided farms between ten and 80 acres for larger families.

The state of Utah

In 1848, the US government defeated Mexico in war and took some of its land. This included the land around Salt Lake. Young wanted to found a Mormon state called Deseret, but the government refused. Young and the government came to a compromise – the territory of Utah was created and, although it was not Mormon, Young was its governor and his word was the law.

Gradually, the Mormons moved throughout Utah. Whenever a new town was set up, an advance party prepared the land by organising irrigation and marking the land. Settlers were chosen carefully so that there were people who could farm, but also people who were shopkeepers, and craftsmen like blacksmiths, who would support the farmers and the production of food.

The Perpetual Emigration Fund

A Perpetual Emigration Fund was established to encourage more Mormons to come to Utah. Mormon missionaries converted people around the world and arranged for them to emigrate to join the faithful. This brought thousands of converts every year, and allowed the Church to extend its influence even further.

The Mountain Meadow Massacre

However, Mormons were still unpopular. Non-Mormons were prejudiced against them and spread rumours that the Mormons were plotting to kill all non-Mormons. In the Mountain Meadow Massacre, a group of emigrants heading to California passed through Utah. They abused the Indians and shouted insults at the Mormons. This provoked the Indians who killed seven of the emigrants. The Indians told the Mormons who decided that in order to prevent the news of the killings getting out, they would have to shoot all the emigrants. The Mormons spread the story that the Indians killed them all, but no one believed them. Events such as these led to the US government replacing Young as the governor of Utah in 1858, though Young remained in control of all the Mormons.

Utah becomes a state

By 1890, Utah had become a state in the United States of America. However, this did not happen until the Mormons agreed to a ban on polygamy.

Examiner's tip

Joseph Smith founded the Mormons; Brigham Young made the religion last. In the exam, a common question is to compare the two leaders of the Mormons, and their successes.

It is not simply a question of choosing one over the other and saying one failed, the other succeeded. You will need to weigh up the successes and failures of both before you come to a conclusion.

There is no right or wrong conclusion. What matters is that you use your knowledge to support your conclusion.

Revision task

Using the information on pages 78–81, complete a chart like this to compare the leadership of the two men.

	Joseph Smith	Brigham Young
Strengths and successes		
Weaknesses and failures		

Exam practice

1. Briefly describe the problems faced by the early settlers on their journey west. **[5]**

2. Explain why the Mormons went west to settle at Salt Lake. **[7]**

Answers online

2.3 Why did people settle in the West? The homesteaders, railroads, and law and order

After gold was discovered in California in the 1840s, many more people decided to move west to find their fortune. The income that came from mining allowed railroads (railways) to be built across the continent and that in turn meant that many more people could travel across North America. Once California and Oregon became heavily populated, many homesteaders began to settle and farm on the Plains.

The difference between the first wave, pioneers, and the second wave, homesteaders, is that **the homesteaders actually settled on the Great Plains**. In just 30 years, much of the most habitable land was taken by the homesteaders from the eastern states.

Focus points

- Why did people move west to become homesteaders in the late 1860s and 1870s?
- How did the homesteaders react to the many problems facing them on the Plains?
- What was life like for women on the homesteads?
- How important were railroads and railroad companies in opening up the West?
- How successful were the government and local people in establishing law and order in the mining towns?

Revision task

This famous picture sums up the idea of 'manifest destiny'. The settlers are taking over the continent step by step, building settlements and farms, while the Indians look on (engulfed by the smoke from the train!).

Make notes around this picture to explain what impression it gives you of the settlement of the West. Comment on each of the features indicated.

Source A: *A painting called 'Westward the Course of Empire Takes Its Way', 1868. It has appeared in more history books in the USA than any other image, and has shaped the way generations of Americans have viewed westward expansion.*

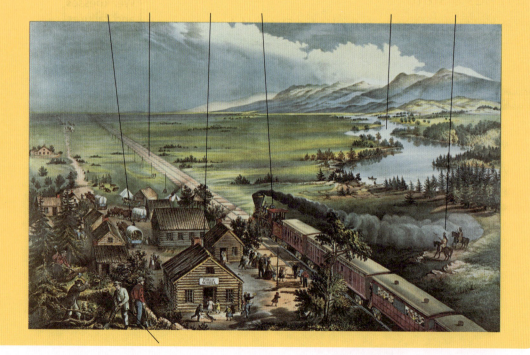

Why did people move west to become homesteaders in the late 1860s and 1870s?

Revised ☐

PUSH FACTORS	PULL FACTORS
Poverty and unemployment in the East: Immigration from Europe increased as people sought their fortune in the USA. Events such as the Irish potato famine in 1848 added to the numbers of immigrants. This led to overcrowding, a shortage of farmland and unemployment in the East.	**US government:** The US government wanted loyal US citizens to settle all over North America, to take control and stop other countries such as Britain from taking over these areas. They encouraged settlement through the idea of **manifest destiny**.
Far western states were heavily populated: California and Oregon were becoming full of people and it was becoming harder to settle and make a life there. The Plains were the only large area left.	**Offer of free land:** The government surveyed all the land in the USA and divided it into areas 9.6 km² in size which could be bought cheaply by anyone ($1 an acre). Land speculators made money by buying land cheaply from the government and then selling it on for large profits. This led to the **Homestead Act** in 1862, which allowed people to claim land for free providing they lived and worked on it for five years. Further acts such as the **Timber and Culture Act** and the **Desert Land Act** made it even easier to claim free land.
The **American Civil War** and the ending of slavery meant that there were many former soldiers and slaves who wanted to make a new life somewhere else.	**Manifest destiny:** All people of the United States believed that they had the right to all land in North America. They saw their government and their good Christian way of life as perfect and it was their duty and God's will to spread this across all of North America. The 'savage' Indians had no right to the land as they had wasted it, and the USA would bring them civilisation.
Persecution: Jews and other religious groups were being mistreated or harassed in Europe and wanted to move somewhere else.	**Railroads:** Railroad companies encouraged people to settle on the Plains, and railway transport made it easier.

Key terms

Manifest destiny – belief among people of the USA in the nineteenth century that they had the God-given right to settle the entire continent

Homestead Act 1862 – law passed to allow settlers to get land for free providing they lived on it for more than five years

Timber and Culture Act 1873 – law passed which gave settlers more free land if they planted a number of trees on it

Desert Land Act 1877 – further allocation of free land in areas where there was a desert and not enough water

American Civil War – the war between the slave-owning Southern states and the Northern states of the USA, which lasted from 1861 to 1865

Revision task

Read the table of push and pull factors on these two pages. Draw your own table and make notes.

Use highlighters to show the different factors as follows:

economic

social

spiritual/religious

Examiner's tip

You don't need to learn all the table but make sure you can remember **at least two** push factors and **two** pull factors.

How did the homesteaders react to the many problems facing them on the Plains?

Revised ☐

PROBLEM: Lack of wood The Plains were grasslands and there was **not much wood** to build houses or provide fuel.

SOLUTION: Homesteaders built **sod houses** from sods of earth which they dug out of the ground. Cattle and buffalo dung was used as fuel.

PROBLEM: Ploughing the land The Plains had never ever been ploughed, so the ground was tough. The machines that had been used in the East broke when they tried to plough the land on the Plains. Farmers could not afford new ones. And, unlike in the Eastern states, there were no farm labourers available to the farmers living on the Plains.

SOLUTION: In the 1880s, stronger and affordable **machines** were mass produced. Homesteaders would also work together to buy machinery in a group, rather than bearing the cost individually.

PROBLEM: Lack of water In winter, the temperature was as low as –40°C, and in the summer it was over 25°C. In the winter, the frozen soil did not let in any water, and in summer the rain evaporated rather than went into the soil. Irrigation was impossible as there were not enough rivers or lakes on the Plains.

SOLUTION: Dry farming – when it rained in summer, or snowed in winter, the land would be ploughed straight away to cover over the moisture to trap it and stop it evaporating.

PROBLEM: Reaching water supplies Wells were expensive and needed to be very deep to reach deep underground supplies.

SOLUTION: The development of **wind pumps** by cattlemen and railroad companies meant that water deep below the surface could be pumped to the surface. This water could be used in people's homes and also to irrigate their crops.

PROBLEM: Landholdings too small The landholding that had been offered to the farmers by the government in the 1860s did not support a family. An average holding was 160 acres but this did not support a family on the Plains.

SOLUTION: The government passed **new Acts** that allowed more land to be claimed by farmers.

PROBLEM: Wrong crops The usual crops that were used elsewhere in the country – corn in the winter and wheat in the spring – could not survive the extreme temperatures and low rainfall.

SOLUTION: In 1874 a **new variety of wheat** was brought from Russia. It was called Turkey Red and survived the climate of the Plains.

PROBLEM: Cost of fencing Farmers needed to fence the land so that they were sure where the boundaries of their holding were and to stop cattle from straying onto their land and eating their crops, but this was expensive and time-consuming.

SOLUTION: The development of **barbed wire** in the 1890s by Joseph Glidden allowed farmers to fence their land quickly and efficiently. This meant animal breeding could take place.

PROBLEMS WITH NO SOLUTIONS:

- **Fire** was a danger in the summer and autumn (usually from lightning strikes).
- In 1874–77, Rocky Mountain **locusts** swarmed through the Plains, eating everything in their path and destroying the farmers' crops.

Examiner's tip

The first railroad across the continent was completed in the 1860s. The railroad affects many aspects of the history of the American West. Look for this symbol to highlight examples of the impact of the railroad:

It was much easier to bring heavy machinery to the Plains after the railroad was built.

Revision task

Make up a table of problems and solutions. To help you remember them, draw or stick in little pictures next to each problem/solution – the sillier they are, the better you will remember them!

For example:
PROBLEM

no wood

SOLUTION:

burnt dung for fuel

Examiner's tip

There are often questions in the exam about the problems for homesteaders. These will be fairly straightforward. But you must know your facts **and** be able to give examples. For the exam, make sure you can remember at least **five** problems and their solutions.

What was life like for women on the homesteads?

Revised

Women had to cook and clean:

- **Cooking** was hard as fuel was difficult to find and they had only limited kinds of food that they could use in their cooking – meals were boring.
- **Cleaning** was difficult. Houses made from mud (sod houses) were dirty, and women needed to clean them constantly with homemade soap, water, rags and brushes made from twigs.

Women had to look after the sick: There were few doctors, and women used natural remedies to treat the sick and injured, as there was little medicine available.

Women had to produce children: Children were needed so that they could help with farming the land, and then continue the farming when their parents became too old to work on the land.

Women were teachers: There were few teachers and they were poorly paid, but they would insist on certain standards of behaviour and did a great deal to civilise the West. It is often said that through this, and their role in the family, the women living on the Plains did as much to bring law and order to society as the sheriffs and the marshals!

Women also had to do farm work: Especially if their husbands were away or died, women did farm work such as tilling, weeding, picking crops and caring for animals.

How important were railroads and railroad companies in opening up the West?

Revised

Why was a railroad built? The US government had wanted to build a railroad linking the west and the east coasts for a long time. The mining boom allowed it to happen. Gold miners (see page 86) needed to bring their valuable gold cargo back from the mines in California to the eastern states. They had the wealth to put into the creation of the railroads that would help them to transport their gold. Two companies started building, one from the west and one from the East. They met in Utah in 1869.

How did it open up the West?

- Even while it was being built it encouraged settlers. The railroad companies were given land by the government to build their railroad. In turn, they sold the land on either side of the railroad to help them pay for the construction work. The railroad advertised its land for sale across North America and as far away as Europe.
- Once it was completed, as well as cargo trains, there were passenger trains for people to travel from one side of the country to the other, passing quickly through the mountains and the grasslands, which had previously been such a barrier.
- Wherever a station was built along the railroad, a town developed, which was a place for homesteaders to buy and sell goods.
- The railroad provided homesteaders with a way to transport supplies and machinery, and this in turn encouraged more people to farm and settle in the Plains.

> **Examiner's tip**
>
> The railroad comes into many aspects of the history of the American West. It was the single most important factor in helping the West to be settled. You will need to refer to it when answering questions in the exam about cattlemen, the struggle for the Plains, law and order as well as the early settlers.
>
>

Revised

Revision task

For your exam, you may be asked about how important the railroad was in opening up the West. Complete the table below. Add more rows if you can.

What the railroad did in the West	How this helped to open up the West	How important (mark out of 10)
Provided cheap land	Encouraged more people to settle on the Plains	
Transported people		
Towns grew up around stations		
Transported heavy farming equipment		

How successful were the government and local people in establishing law and order in the mining towns?

The discovery of gold

In 1848, gold was discovered in California. Within months, 40,000 men crossed the Plains to get from the east coast to California with the sole aim of staking a claim to land in which they would find gold and make their fortunes. Almost as many men took a sea route round from the east to the west coast. Some of the men travelling across did not survive the journey, and many others failed to find gold and so made their way back home to the East.

In later years, gold was discovered in many other places in the West and on the Plains, for example in Idaho in 1860 and in the Black Hills of Dakota in 1874. Each time, miners flocked to the area in large numbers.

The development of mining towns

In the early stages, miners lived in temporary camps. These grew and disappeared quickly.

Around the 1850s, the surface mining had run out and so, to reach the gold that was deep in the mines, miners had to become more professional. They would be backed by businessmen from the eastern states and they started to live in more permanent settlements. This trend was speeded up by the development of the railroad, as cargo trains helped to move out the silver and gold, and bring in food and supplies to the miners.

Crime

Crime was a major concern in mining areas. The main crimes were:

- **Gunslingers and gangs:** Banks held large amounts of cash to buy gold from the miners. Before the railroad was developed, this money was taken to the banks in stagecoaches. The coaches were a really easy target for gangs of bank robbers or lone gunslingers, for example Jesse James.

- **Stealing:** Miners would steal gold or money from each other.

Examiner's tip

Questions about law and order may relate to two different areas: the mining towns and the cow towns (see page 88). Some of the issues are the same for both types of town; some are different.

- **Claim jumping:** Miners could 'stake a claim' to an area of land by hammering wooden stakes into the ground and then registering this claim. If gold was discovered, then someone might steal the claim by stealing the stake or the land.
- **Shooting:** Everyone carried guns and so it was common for disputes to end in a shooting.

Establishing law and order

To start with, there were no US government law officers, so it was up to the local people to deal with these crimes.

Miner courts: Disputes about claims were dealt with by a committee of miners. A sheriff was appointed to deal with law breakers and a court of all the miners would decide on the punishment. Common punishments were flogging, banishment or hanging. However, these were not effective as the sheriff and the courts were easily influenced – sheriffs could be threatened or bribed and courts took a long time to dispense justice.

Vigilantes: Vigilantes became popular in mining towns – they were a group of people or one person who were not official but claimed to uphold law and order and deal with suspected wrongdoers. They did not take the suspect to a court but instead dealt with them quickly, usually by hanging the person. It could be very effective. For example, in Bannock, a mining town in Montana, the people were terrorised by a gang of 100 men. The vigilantes hunted down and then hanged the leader of the gang (who was the town sheriff!) and the gang disappeared. However, many people feared the vigilantes because they often ignored evidence so that they could deal with the 'criminals' quickly. Their rapid decisions sometimes meant that they hanged the wrong person, often at a 'neck-tie' party.

Revision task

Write down the advantages and disadvantages of vigilantes. Then come to your own conclusion about how successful they were in keeping law and order.

Exam practice

1. Study Source A (on page 82). What can you learn from this source about life in the American West? **[5]**
2. Briefly describe the work of vigilantes. **[5]**
3. Did Mormons and homesteaders move west for the same reasons? **[8]**

Answers online

Key term

Claim jumping – stealing someone else's land or mining stake

Examiner's tip

When you get a question about law and order in the exam, remember to think about what was a threat to ordinary people in their day-to-day lives. For miners, claim jumping was much more important than any other crime.

Ordinary people in the West were often jealous of banks which held all the money as they struggled to survive. Gunfighters and bank robbers like Jesse James were often seen as heroes (a bit like Robin Hood).

Key term

Vigilantes – people who took the law into their own hands; often they **lynched** (hanged) someone without a trial

Examiner's tip

If you are asked a question about law and order in a mining town, remember to mention vigilantes. When mining towns first developed, vigilantes were the only way in which people could get justice, because there were no law officers. Gradually, the influence of sheriffs on law and order increased as communication improved.

2.4 What were the consequences of the spread of cattle ranching to the Plains?

Focus points

- How and why did cattle ranching spread from Texas to the Great Plains?
- What was life like for a cowboy?
- Why were there problems of law and order in the cow towns?
- Why did ranchers and homesteaders come into conflict with each other? (Case study: the Johnson County War)
- Why did the open range end by the 1890s?

How and why did cattle ranching spread from Texas to the Great Plains?

Revised

Cattle ranching in Texas

- Spanish invaders first brought cattle to America in the 1500s.
- The cattle thrived, particularly in southern Texas which had a **mild climate** with **plenty of water.**
- The **cattle roamed wild** – there were no fences. This type of ranching was called the **open range**. The **cattle ranchers** employed Indians to round up the cattle for their meat.
- As the population of the northern states of the USA grew so did the **demand for beef**. Texan ranchers drove their cattle north to sell them. This was called the **Long Drive**.
- The Plains Indians would demand payment for cattle drives crossing their land.

Key terms

Open range – a large area of unfenced land on which cattle can graze

Cattle ranchers – people who own (or manage) large farms (ranches) where cattle are bred

Long Drive – movement of cattle from the open range in Texas to the markets (and, later, to railheads)

A boom industry!

From the late 1860s cattle ranching boomed for two main reasons:

- **The Civil War**: During the 1860s the north and the south of the USA fought a Civil War. The cattle trade was disrupted. Cattle were not killed so **the number of cattle grew dramatically**. When Texas rancher Charles Goodnight went away to fight in the war he had 180 cattle. When he came back he had 5000! Other ranchers found the same. There were a quarter of a million excess cattle in Texas in the 1860s. The ranchers knew that if they could get these cattle north they could **make a fortune**.
- The **growth of railroads** gave cattle ranching a further boost. The cattle could be transported even further to the people living in the eastern states. In 1869 the transcontinental railroad connected the entire continent – east to west.

Revision task

Add ranching to the chart you made on page 86 to summarise the impact of railroads on the settlement of the West.

Cow towns

The railroads also led to the development of cow towns.

Joseph McCoy was a cattle dealer. He established a town called **Abilene** by building offices and cattle pens next to a **railhead** where the southern cattle drivers could meet up with the northern cattle buyers. Between 1867 and 1881, half a million cattle passed through Abilene.

Other cow towns were established along the railroad, such as Dodge City, Wichita and Ellsworth.

Conflict with homesteaders

The map shows you the different cattle trails used for the long drive to the railheads and cow towns. Some of these crossed land being farmed by homesteaders. This caused conflict.

- The homesteaders feared that the Texan cattle would bring **diseases** to their own livestock.
- The cattle used up their **precious supplies of water**.

Homesteaders joined together to block the cattle trails.

Ranching begins on the Plains

With homesteaders and the Indians making driving cattle difficult, some ranchers started ranching on the Great Plains where they could be in easy reach of the railheads and cow towns.

John Iliff was one of the first to make a success of ranching on the Plains. He bought a herd of cattle from **Oliver Loving** in 1866 and kept them on the Plains.

- He made money by supplying beef to the Union Pacific Railroad Construction Group.
- In 1872 he supplied Red Cloud and the Sioux reservations.
- He also transported slaughtered cattle to the east in refrigerated railroad carts.

In 1880, **Charles Goodnight** began ranching in Colorado. Other ranchers followed his example. By the late 1880s the Long Drive from Texas to the north had all but ended.

The ranchers brought the same **open range** practice to the Great Plains as they had used in Texas.

- They did not buy the land their cattle grazed on – ranchers could not afford to.
- Even if they owned land, they could not fence it all so the cattle ignored boundaries and roamed wherever they wanted to.
- To identify their cattle, they had them **branded**. Any calves stayed with the mother's owner as it was impossible to find out who the father bull was (and its owner).

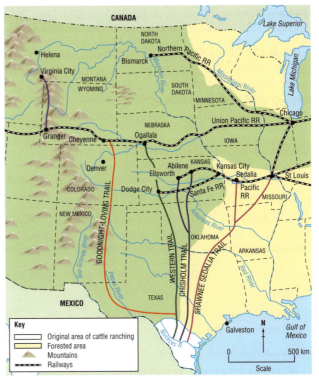

↑ **A map of the Plains showing the main cattle trails**

What was life like for a cowboy?

Who were cowboys? Many were ex-soldiers from the Civil War; 25 per cent were black freed slaves; 12 per cent were Mexican.

Where did cowboys live? They lived in a dug-out or a shack. When ranching replaced the Long Drive, they lived in ranch houses.

What work did cowboys do?

- Their main job was to look after the cattle on the open range.
- Once a year the cowboys rounded up the cattle and branded the new calves with the sign for their cattlemen or ranch.

The Long Drive

- In spring, the cattle were rounded up in Texas to be driven to market.
- The herd had to be guarded 24 hours a day as they were very valuable, so the cowboys slept with the herd.
- About 10 to 14 cowboys would drive the 3000 or so cattle.
- **Natural hazards: stampedes**, crossing rivers, scorpions, snakes and quicksand; extreme weather on the Plains.
- **Danger from people:** Indians or **cattle rustlers** might steal the cattle; some cowboys were killed by Indians raiding their cattle.
- **At the end of a long drive**, cowboys took their payment and were let loose from the responsibility of looking after the herd. They had spent months of hard work looking after their cattle, and were looking for fun. They spent their money on new clothes and a shave, but also on drinking, in gambling halls and in brothels.

Once **fenced ranching** replaced the Long Drive and the open range, cowboys became much more like farmhands.

Key terms

Stampede – when cattle were out of control and ran as a herd; this was lethal as they could trample a person to death

Cattle rustling – stealing cattle

Revision task

In the middle of a piece of paper, draw a sketch of a cowboy with all the equipment in the table below. Name each piece of equipment and use one or two key words to sum up why a cowboy needed it.

Equipment	Why a cowboy needed it to do his job
Hat	Known as a Stetson, the hat was the cowboy's 'roof' against the weather – sun, rain and snow.
Bandana	This was worn around the neck like a scarf. It could be used to protect the back of the neck from the sun, to tie on the hat in windy weather, as a dust mask, an ear cover in cold weather, a towel, a blindfold for nervous horses, a strainer for muddy water, a dish-dryer, a sling or bandage, an aid for hand signalling and for tying a calf's legs together.
Lariat	Made from thin leather, this was essential for catching and working with the cattle.
Boots	These had a high heel to keep the foot in the stirrup and were always worn with spurs.
Gloves	These protected the hands, which could be rubbed raw when using the lariat.
Saddle	This was the cowboy's essential piece of equipment. Without it he could not do his job and so it was his most prized possession.
Six-shooter	The six-shooter or revolver was the essential status symbol of the cowboy. Few cowboys were very accurate with it. Often it would be left in the chuck (food) wagon.
Chaps	These were made from leather and designed to protect the legs from thorny vegetation, from chafing on a long ride, and to give some protection in a fall.

Why were there problems of law and order in the cow towns?

Some crimes were **similar to those in mining towns** (see page 87) for example: bank robbery; train/stagecoach robbery; and shootings (most people owned guns).

However, there were other crimes that particularly affected the cattle industry.

- **Cattle rustling:** Herds of cattle on the open range were an easy target for rustlers. Branding marks were altered.
- **Fence cutting:** Homesteaders and small ranchers cut the fences owned by rich and powerful cattlemen.
- **Horse stealing:** This was regarded as a serious crime because horses were so valuable for life in the West. Horse stealers were often hanged if convicted. This clashed with the attitudes of the Plains Indians who believed that horse stealing was a way that warriors gained honour.

There were also tensions between different groups of people that could easily spill over into violence:

- between ranchers and homesteaders over cattle roaming on farmland
- between races. Many different races worked or settled on the Plains. As well as the Indians and the white settlers there were Chinese railway builders and miners; black homesteaders; black and Mexican cowboys.
- between cowboys and townspeople when hundreds of cowboys were let loose on the town at the end of the long drive.

Who kept law and order in the cow towns?

Cow towns sprang up quickly. The government did not send officials to keep law and order. To start with it was up to the towns to organise this themselves.

- **Marshals** were appointed by the people in the town.
- **Sheriffs** covered a county. They were elected by the people.
- There were also **vigilantes** in cow towns just as there were in mining towns (see page 87).

Example: Wild Bill Hickock

- Hickock was a soldier in the American Civil War. He then served under General Custer.
- After this, he became famous as a gunfighter. He duelled in daylight with a man who he had quarrelled with about a game of cards. He gained a reputation as a man who had killed a lot of men.
- In 1868, Hickok became sheriff of Hays City in Kansas. He used violence and threats to bring the town under control. He was so violent that he was ousted and replaced by his deputy.
- In April 1871, Hickok was employed as marshal of Abilene. He did not take his job very seriously, and spent most of his time playing poker.

Examiner's tip

Remember these examples of crimes in mining/cow towns.

Similar

Crimes such as racial attacks and shootings were common to both types of town.

Different

MINING TOWNS: Claim jumping (stealing claims to gold)

COW TOWNS: Cattle rustling, fence cutting, horse stealing.

Examiner's tip

You don't need to know the story of Hickock in detail. It is simply an example of how law and order was maintained in the towns of the American West by sheriffs and marshals.

Revision task

As railroads developed, US government officials could travel more easily to new towns. This helped solve the problem of a lack of law officers in mining towns and cow towns. Add this to your 'impact of railways' chart.

Why did ranchers and homesteaders come into conflict with each other?

Before the 1870s, during the era of the cattle drives, the homesteaders' main fear was that their livestock might catch a **disease** from the ranchers' cattle, or that the cattle might **damage** their crops. They blocked the ranchers from driving their cattle through their land.

From the 1870s, once ranching moved onto the Plains, ranchers and homesteaders were now **competing for the same land** and for power.

1880s: Tensions in Johnson County

In the 1870s cattlemen settled in Wyoming. Some set up huge ranches in Johnson County. These powerful 'cattle barons' formed the **Wyoming Stock Grower's Association** which passed laws protecting their interests.

In the 1880s homesteaders and smaller ranchers settled in Wyoming. There were soon disputes over land. People settled on land that the barons claimed as theirs. There were more homesteaders than cattlemen, but the barons were richer and more powerful.

Tensions rose further in the 1880s for other reasons:

- Beef **prices** were **falling**.
- **Droughts** and **harsh winters** killed some of the cattle.
- Some **ranchers went bankrupt** and lost their land, which homesteaders were quick to take for their own.
- Homesteaders **fenced off water holes** that ranchers needed for their cattle to drink from.

However the cattle barons' greatest concern was **cattle rustling**. The barons accused the homesteaders of stealing their cattle. As they did not trust a jury of local men to convict the rustlers, they hired a gunfighter to **hunt down the rustlers**.

1889: The lynching of Averill and Watson

Jim Averill ran a small store, post office and saloon. He was a critic of the cattle barons. He had publicly called them land-grabbers. **Ella Watson**, his partner, was a prostitute. Cowboys often paid for Ella's services by giving her a cow.

Bothwell, a cattle baron, claimed that Averill and Watson were living on his land. He also accused

them of cattle rustling. He formed a **vigilance committee**, who lynched them both.

1892: The Johnson County War

In **April 1892**, the homesteaders decided to round up all of the cattle on the open range in Johnson County, partly to sort out who owned which cattle, but also to stop the cattle wandering over the homesteaders' farmland. The cattle barons believed that more of their cattle would be rustled, so they came up with a plan.

The plan

- The Wyoming Stock Growers' Association (ranchers/cattle barons) drew up a list of 70 people they believed were rustlers.
- They formed a vigilance committee, called the **Regulators**, who hired 24 Texan gunfighters and headed for Johnson County, taking along two newspaper reporters to report on what they were doing.
- Their plan was to capture the town of Buffalo, kill the sheriff of Johnson County (Red Angus) and then kill the rest of the men on their list.

What happened

- On their way to Buffalo, the Regulators came to a ranch owned by Nate Champion. He held them off until they burnt him out of his cabin and killed him and his friend Nick Ray.
- However, the alarm had been raised in Buffalo. Next day, as the Regulators approached town, they heard that the local people were armed and ready.
- They retreated to another ranch, where they were surrounded by Red Angus and nearly 300 homesteaders.
- One of the Regulators managed to escape and persuaded the US Cavalry to come to their rescue.
- The Regulators were charged with murder but bribed the jury with money and were let off.

Consequences

- **Short term**: the cattle barons were widely condemned. They lost a lot of their power and influence in Wyoming. Meanwhile, the homesteaders could carry on with their lives.
- **Long term**: the open range ended.

Why did the open range end by the 1890s?

Revised ☐

1880–85

- **OVERGRAZING**: ranching made lots of money, so more people became ranchers. By 1882 there were too many cattle and **not enough grass** to feed them.
- **BAD WEATHER**: A **drought** in 1883 withered the grass.
- **FALLING BEEF PRICES**: Supply outstripped demand so ranchers earned less for their cattle.

↓

1885–87

- **MORE BAD WEATHER**: Cattle need good grass; good grass needs good weather. Two very cold winters and a hot, dry summer killed grass and many cattle

↓

1890s

- **CATTLE RUSTLING**: Protecting cattle was almost impossible on the open range.
- **UNEMPLOYMENT**: As ranching hit problems some ranchers went bankrupt; others cut back and laid off cowboys.

The end of the open range

The cattlemen realised that they needed to **look after their cattle and the grass**, so they began to **fence off their own land**. This meant they could:

- breed their cattle selectively to produce better meat or more milk
- use wind pumps to get water from deep in the ground
- grow better grass to feed their cattle.

2.5 Why did white Americans and the Plains Indians find it so difficult to reach a peaceful settlement of their differences?

There is really only one main answer to this question – **LAND**. The white Americans and the Indians had very different attitudes to land:

> **White Americans** believed they had a right to settle wherever they wanted to across North America, and that it was their manifest destiny – their God-given duty – to do so.

> **Plains Indians** believed that land was sacred and shouldn't belong to anyone, shouldn't be bought or sold. They believed that they were connected to nature, and connected to the land.

These differences weren't a problem while the white Americans thought that the Plains were a desert – they were happy for the Plains Indians to carry on living there. However, when it became clear that people could settle and prosper on the Plains the white Americans began to see the Indians as a problem. The white Americans wanted to settle on the Plains and the Plains Indians were getting in their way.

Focus points

- Did all white Americans have the same attitudes towards the Plains Indians?
- Why did white Americans and Plains Indians come into conflict?
- Why did the policy of the American government towards the Plains Indians change so often between 1840 and 1868?
- Why did the Plains Indians win the Battle of the Little Bighorn?
- How important was the Battle of the Little Bighorn in the eventual defeat of the Plains Indians?
- What was the purpose and effect of the reservations?

Did all white Americans have the same attitudes towards the Plains Indians?

Revised ☐

From the 1840s onwards, the Plains Indians were occupying land that settlers, miners and ranchers wanted. The white Americans did not understand the Indians. They **saw the Indians as savages because of their different beliefs and values**, such as exposure, polygamy and scalping.

There were two different attitudes among the white Americans about what should happen to the Indians:

> **Key term**
>
> **Reservations** – areas of land set aside by the US government for Indians to live on

> **Negotiators:** These were mainly people living in the East. Some of them may have never met an Indian although some were government officials who would have worked with the Indians and gained some understanding of their way of life. They believed that **aggressive tactics would make matters worse**. Instead, they believed that through **education, missionary work and settlement** onto **reservations** they would turn the Indians **into model citizens**.

> **Exterminators:** These people mainly lived in the Plains – settlers, miners, ranchers – and had the most to gain if the **Indians** were **removed**. They were the people who were most likely to have had hostile contact with the Indians. They believed that the only solution would be if all Plains Indians were **destroyed**.

Why did white Americans and Plains Indians come into conflict?

The white Americans wanted to settle and farm the Plains, while the Indians wanted to maintain their ancient way of life of following the buffalo across the Plains. Below are the events which show increasing conflict between them.

Revision task

1. For the exam, you need to know these events in order and in detail, and be able to see the patterns in them. Create a timeline from 1825 to 1890. Summarise the key events from the information below. Add any extra information that you remember from your lessons.

   Add small drawings to help you remember the different events. Refer back to it when you revise the American West.

2. Highlight events in your timeline that show the following causes at work:
   - ☐ breaking treaties
   - ☐ desire for land
   - ☐ gold
   - ☐ Indians attacking
   - ☐ army attacking.

   Use a different colour/highlight for each, and create a key so that you have a visual idea of the factors that answer the key question: Why did white Americans and Plains Indians come into conflict?

1825–40: **The Great Plains were seen as a desert by non-Indians**

1832: The Great Plains were set aside as Indian country, with the **Permanent Indian Frontier**.

1840–50: **White Americans crossed the Plains – limited conflict**

The early pioneers crossed the Plains to get to California and Oregon. Indians sometimes **attacked** the emigrants, but they also **traded** with them or even **guided** them.

1848: Gold was discovered in California.

1850–59: **Settlers began to come to the Plains – increasing conflict**

Miners crossed Cheyenne and Arapaho land to get to the gold mines in California. On their way, they killed the buffalo, and brought disease and whisky to the Plains Indians.

1851: The Fort Laramie Treaty between the Plains Indians and the US Government. Special areas of land were set apart for each nation of Plains Indians to live and hunt in. These were away from the settler trails and the treaty said that the Indians would not be disturbed.

The **railroad** started to develop and settlers began to come to the Plains.

1859: Gold was discovered in many areas of land that had been designated for the Indians. The government had no control over the miners as they rushed to these areas to make their fortunes.

1859–69: **Serious conflict**

1861: Indians began serious attacks on the miners, settlers and railroad surveyors. They refused to obey their chiefs who had made treaties with the US Government.

1864: The Sand Creek Massacre. Cheyenne and Arapaho men, women and children were massacred by the US cavalry as they were surrendering. More women and children were killed than warriors. The leader of the soldiers, John Chivington, infamously said of his actions, 'nits make lice'. He meant that he aimed to kill the children so that they did not grow up to be adult warriors fighting against the cavalry. For the first time, public opinion among white Americans turned in favour of the Indians. People in the East were angry with what the army had done. However, this was only temporary.

1865–68: Red Cloud's War

- **Gold was discovered** in Montana in 1862, an area that had been designated for the Sioux Indians.
- A new trail called **the Bozeman Trail** went directly through Sioux land and broke the peace treaty. The Sioux attacked the people who travelled along the Bozeman Trail for a year, while the army tried to negotiate peace with the Sioux leader, Red Cloud. The army built a chain of forts along the trail.
- In **1866** the army were under siege in their forts. The Sioux killed 80 men led by Captain Fetterman trying to escape Fort Kearney. No travellers could use the Bozeman Trail.
- In **1868**, the US Government negotiated another Fort Laramie Treaty. The army withdrew from the Bozeman Trail, and the Indians moved onto the Great Sioux Reservation, which would be an area where no non-Indians would be allowed to settle. Red Cloud agreed to this treaty.

1869–1878: Final conflict on the Plains

1874: Gold was discovered in the Black Hills. This was the **most sacred area of land for the Sioux** – the higher the land, the more sacred it was – and was central to the Great Sioux Reservation. The Black Hills were invaded by miners – the government could not stop this, and they did not want to. The government offered to buy the land from the Sioux for $6,000,000, but the Sioux did not believe that sacred land should be bought or sold and rejected the offer.

1876: The Great Sioux War began. The Sioux, the Arapaho and the Cheyenne were angry about the Black Hills being invaded and some of them would not return to their reservations. In June, this led to the **Battle of the Little Bighorn**, and the defeat of General Custer and the Seventh Cavalry (see page 97). But the victory was temporary.

1877–1890: The defeat of the Plains Indians

January 1877: The hero of the Battle of the Little Bighorn, Sitting Bull, left the Plains. He tried to make money by working in a Wild West show, but eventually returned to join the reservation.

1879: The Sioux were given **cattle** and had to live off them to survive on the reservations.

By 1883: The white Americans had hunted the buffalo virtually into extinction. At the same time the **Bureau of Indian Affairs** banned customs like the Sun Dance.

By 1885: All Indians were on reservations.

In 1887, these were divided by the **Dawes Act** so they were not owned by the entire tribe or nation.

1889: The Oklahoma Land Run. Land that had previously been given to the Indians was split into 160-acre plots under the Homestead Act – 2 million acres were claimed in 24 hours in April.

1890: A medicine man called Wovoka had a vision that if Indians wore certain ceremonial clothing and danced in a certain way they would be impossible to kill and their way of life (including the buffalo) would come back. This **Ghost Dance** spread through all reservations and terrified the government. Sitting Bull was killed during the attempt to arrest him. Sioux Chief Big Foot led his people to **Wounded Knee Creek**, where they were massacred by the US Army.

Why did the policy of the American government towards the Plains Indians change so often between 1840 and 1868?

Revised ☐

The settlement of the Plains was not planned. Americans may have believed it was their manifest destiny to inhabit the whole of the continent but they did not set out with a master plan for doing it!

Instead the government responded to circumstances. As the circumstances changed so did their policy towards the Indians. In particular:

● **Land**: When no white Americans wanted the Plains they were happy for the Indians to live there. Once settlers wanted the land for farming they changed their policy.	● **Gold**: Each phase of the conflict was triggered by the discovery of gold: first in California; then in Montana; finally in the Black Hills. Before gold was discovered the government promised the Indians they would be left alone. Once gold was discovered they supported the claims of the miners because it made the USA more wealthy.
● **Railways**: In the early period travel across the continent was hard. Only the bravest would try to cross the Plains and the mountains. The Indians were left alone. Once the transcontinental railway was built in the 1860s the entire continent was accessible. Now the Indians were seen as a problem.	● **Indian Wars**: In the early decades the Indians were not seen as a military threat. The 'negotiators' set the policy. But, once some of the Indian nations began to fight back and win, the government attitude changed. The 'exterminators' set the policy.

And remember:

● **Control**: The US government did not really control much of the West. A lot of the time it was the miners, homesteaders or the ranchers – the settlers in the West – who were dictating policy to the government rather than the other way round. The government were happy to leave it like that. They would rather the land be controlled by loyal white settlers than the Indians. So if settlers broke a treaty with the Indians the government would protect the settlers rather than trying to defend the Treaty and the Indians.

Why did the Plains Indians win the Battle of the Little Bighorn?

Revised ☐

In 1876, all Plains Indians were ordered onto their reservations. However, many of them would not return to them because they were angry about the invasion of the Black Hills. In June, **Sitting Bull** and **Crazy Horse** and 2000 warriors from the Sioux, Cheyenne and Arapaho nations set up camp on the banks of the **Bighorn River**, an area outside of the Great Sioux Reservation. **This was in direct defiance of army orders**, so the army was ordered to attack all Sioux who had not returned to their reservation.

The army planned to attack the camp that the Indians had set up. They planned to trap the Sioux by attacking in three separate columns led by three generals (see diagram 1).

Battle of the Rosebud
On 17 June, Crazy Horse and some warriors attacked General Crook's column and killed or injured 90 soldiers before retreating back to camp. Crook's column was severely weakened and could no longer attack the Indian camp.

> **Examiner's tip**
>
> For the exam, you must make sure that you are clear about
> ● the **events** of the battle,
> ● the **tactics** that were used and
> ● the **mistakes** that the army forces made.

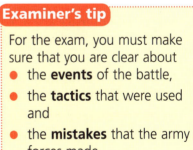

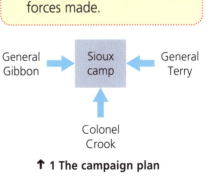

↑ **1 The campaign plan**

Changed tactics
Terry and Gibbon joined forces. They changed tactics (see diagram 2).

- The **Seventh Cavalry**, a small but quick force led by **General Custer**, would attack the Sioux camp from the south.
- Custer was offered extra weapons and men but refused them. The larger troop, with more weapons, would attack from the north.

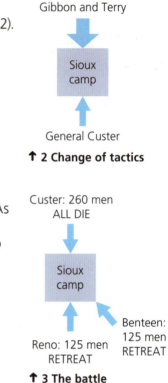

↑ **2 Change of tactics**

↑ **3 The battle**

Battle of the Little Bighorn
Custer and his cavalry travelled by day and night to the Sioux camp. As they were smaller and quicker, **they arrived a day earlier** than the larger troop but **were exhausted**. Custer sent out some scouts who reported that the Indians seemed to be packing up to leave camp, so he decided to attack there and then.

Custer split his small force of 510 men into **three groups** to attack from different sides.

Reno's and Benteen's attacks failed and they retreated. They both realised they could not overcome so many Indians.

Custer carried on. All the Indian warriors were focused on Custer and his small force, now totally outnumbered. They bravely fought on, but all were killed. This was known as **Custer's Last Stand**. Custer's men were scalped or mutilated by the Indians. Custer was not.

Why did the US army LOSE?	Why did the Plains Indians WIN?
<ul><li>Custer's army had **inferior weapons.** The Sioux had faster and better rifles than the soldiers!</li><li>Custer **refused reinforcements** or better weapons because he thought they would slow him down.</li><li>There was **no communication** between Custer, Reno and Benteen.</li><li>They **underestimated** the number of Indian warriors.</li><li>Custer did not make any attempt to hide their attack. The Indians knew that they were coming and were prepared.</li><li>**Custer pushed his men too hard.** They had travelled day and night and were tired.</li><li>**Custer disobeyed orders.** He failed to wait for the larger cavalry and weapons. He wanted all of the glory for himself.</li></ul>	<ul><li>**The Plains Indians were angry.** For 30 years they had been making treaties with the white Americans over land, and these treaties kept getting broken.</li><li>The Indian camp at Little Bighorn was larger than any in American history. The army thought there were 800 warriors, but there were **2000**.</li><li>Crazy Horse and Sitting Bull had had **visions** that they would defeat the men dressed in blue. This meant that they and their followers had total conviction that they would win the battle.</li><li>They led skillfully, for example, **Sitting Bull** made sure that the women and children in the camp were safe so that the warriors could concentrate on fighting rather than worrying about their families. **Crazy Horse** led the warriors in battle fearlessly and with clever tactics.</li></ul>

> **Revision task**
>
> On your own table of the Battle, use a highlighter to divide the reasons for losing/winning into long-term – those which had built up over time (for example, the hatred of white people felt by the Indians) and short-term – those which happened at the time (for example, Custer disobeying orders).

How important was the Battle of the Little Bighorn in the eventual defeat of the Plains Indians?

Revised

The Battle of the Little Bighorn was a victory for the Indians, but it led to a change of opinion in government and a change of tactics, both of which were important in the defeat of the Plains Indians.

Change of opinion – no more negotiation: The news of the 'massacre' at the Little Bighorn reached Washington, the capital of the USA, on 4 July 1876. This was the 100th anniversary of the Declaration of Independence. It was reported as the Indians massacring the army, not as a battle fought between two sides. This was the final straw for some of the public and the people in government who had been negotiators (see page 94). They changed their opinion.

Change of tactic – kill all the buffalo: At the same time, it became more obvious that a direct attack on the Plains Indians would not always work. The army realised that slaughtering the buffalo would be a much more effective way to end the resistance of the Indians. Remember how important the buffalo was to the Indians, not just for their food but in all aspects of their lives (see pages 71–72). In 1840 there were 13 million buffalo on the Plains. By 1885, the buffalo had all been killed. This was because of white Americans successfully hunting the buffalo for sport and for hides but this was deliberately encouraged by the government. The end of the buffalo brought an end to the way of life of the Plains Indians. There was no need to be nomadic to follow the buffalo herds – there were no herds. The joy and excitement of the hunt had gone, and with it the Indians' spirit was broken. With no buffalo the Indians could not survive on the Plains. Defeated and dispirited, they had to move to the reservations.

These changes were important in the defeat of the Plains Indians, but there were **other factors** that were also important:

- **Diseases** the Plains Indians caught from the white Americans, such as smallpox and measles, reduced their numbers and affected their spirits.
- Plains Indian tribes **were divided**. They could not live together in large numbers as they could not hunt enough buffalo to feed everyone. They could only survive when split but were weaker like this.
- The **railroad** could supply and support the army, but the Indians had to use horses and smoke signals instead.
- After the Battle of the Little Bighorn the government no longer supplied the Indians with any weapons and equipment.
- The **reservations** broke the spirit of the Plains Indians.

> **Revision task**
>
> Create a memory map to show the different factors that led to the defeat of the Plains Indians.

> **Examiner's tip**
>
> In your answers about the defeat of the Plains Indians, you must remember the **impact on their spiritual life**. The ending/destruction of the buffalo and the removal of the hunt from the core of their lives meant they had lost everything that they had lived for. It is valid in the exam for you to discuss how the **Plains Indians' loss of self-confidence and self-esteem** was a reason for the way that the Indians lived on the reservations.

What was the purpose and effect of the reservations?

From 1825, Indian reservations were set up on the Great Plains by the US government. They were intended to:

- separate the Indians from the homesteaders and ranchers
- separate Indian nations from each other
- encourage the Indians to become farmers, and therefore become self-sufficient and 'civilised'.

To start with, the Indians could leave the reservations to hunt buffalo, but after the conflict in the 1860s and 1870s, this was banned by the US government. Indian reservations were supervised by government-appointed Indian Agents.

Conditions on the reservations	Effects of the conditions on the Plains Indians
Reservations were set up on land that the settlers didn't want, and so it was of **poor quality** for farming. Also, **the Indians did not know how to farm**.	The Indians did not grow enough to become self-suficient. The Indians became **dependent on handouts for food and clothing**. The lack of food meant they were **hungry** and **ill**. As they had to rely on handouts, rather than hunting for their food, they **lost their status as warriors**.
Feasts, dances and ceremonies such as the Sun Dance were banned.	The young men could not seek visions. **They lost their spiritual lives**, and without the buffalo, they lost their self-belief.
Children in reservations were taken away from their parents to be educated as white children were, and they were taught to speak English.	The children no longer fitted into the Indian world, and **family life was damaged**. Indian customs and traditions used to be spread by talking their language but now children could not share in the culture of their tribe.
Their **horses and weapons were taken away** from them.	They **lost their status** with no horses, and were **unable to fight back** against the white Americans.
The soldiers on the reservations were **violent** and people were **punished harshly** without trial. Both Crazy Horse and Sitting Bull were killed by soldiers on a reservation after being arrested.	This made others **less likely to resist the soldiers** and more likely to obey the rules of the reservations.

The reservations controlled the Plains Indians by destroying their culture. Gradually, the reservations were split up and reduced in size into smaller and smaller areas. The Plains Indians would never again be able to fight back against the white Americans.

Exam practice

1. Why did Indians and white Americans come into conflict? **[5]**

2. Explain why the Indians were able to win the Battle of the Little Bighorn. **[7]**

3. How far was the Battle of the Little Bighorn in 1876 a victory for the Plains Indians? **[8]**

Answers online

3 Germany, c.1919–1945

3.1 Was the Weimar Republic doomed from the start?

By the end of the First World War in 1918, Germany was defeated. The **Allies** would not make peace with Germany unless the country was made more democratic. This meant them getting rid of their **Kaiser**, Wilhelm II, who had most of the power over Germany. So:

- The Kaiser, who had ruled Germany for twenty years, was forced out.
- A new **democratic** government was formed – **the Weimar Republic** – with a new leader – Friedrich Ebert – and a new **constitution** (see page 103).

However, this new government proved unpopular and faced serious problems that soon threatened to destroy the Weimar Republic.

Key issues

- What continuing impact did defeat in the First World War and the Treaty of Versailles have on the Weimar Republic?
- Why was the Republic so unpopular with many Germans?
- How far did life improve for German people 1924–1929?
- What were the achievements of the Weimar period?

Key terms

Allies – countries that have signed an agreement to support each other. (In the First World War, Britain, France and the USA were allies)

Kaiser – Emperor

Democracy – where the people choose the government and opposing views are tolerated

The Weimar Republic – a republic is a country without a hereditary ruler, such as a king or emperor; the new government met in a town called Weimar

Constitution – the rules that decide how a country is governed

What continuing impact did defeat in the First World War and the Treaty of Versailles have on the Weimar Republic?

Revised ☐

- The First World War **killed and injured millions** of Germans.
- The War had **disrupted farming** and the British blockade of German ports had prevented food imports, so food was scarce.
- Demobbed soldiers came home and couldn't get jobs.
- People were starving and thousands died in a **flu epidemic** in 1919.

Key terms

Soviet – a revolutionary council of workers

Dictatorship – a one-party state, governed by an absolute ruler; the opposite of a democracy

Against this background there was:

- **A political revolution** – sailors mutinied in Kiel and set up communist-style **soviets**; the Kaiser was forced to resign and leave the country. A country that had been run like a military **dictatorship** for fifty years now had to learn a different kind of government.

- **Economic chaos** – the government had borrowed so much money to pay for the war that it was **deep in debt**. Factories that had been producing goods for the war now had to get back to making things for **peacetime**. This takes time and money.

- **Depression and division** – before the war Germans had been proud and ambitious. The war left many of them **bitter** and disillusioned. A country once famous for its unity and obedience was now famous for its **squabbling**.

The Treaty of Versailles

With all these problems you'd expect the new government to struggle. But their biggest problem of all was actually the peace treaty they had been forced to sign. The terms were hard on Germany.

LAND

- **Germany lost 13 per cent of its land** (and 6 million people living there).
- It **lost land containing coal** that it needed for industry.
- Germany was **split into two** to give Poland access to the sea (the Polish corridor).
- **German troops were not allowed in the Rhineland** – a **demilitarised** area.
- Germany's **overseas colonies** were given to the Allies.

Key
- Land lost due to Treaty of Versailles
- Demilitarised area

BLAME	ARMY	MONEY
• Germany was **blamed for the war**. • This meant that the **Allies could claim compensation from Germany** for the damage caused by the war.	• **The German army was reduced to 100,000** (it had been 1.75 million). • **The navy was cut to 15,000** – only six battleships were left. • Germany was **not allowed an air force or any tanks or submarines** (new technology).	• **Reparations had to be paid** by Germany to France and Belgium who had been devastated by trench warfare. • In 1921 reparations were set at **£6600 million!**

When the German people saw the terms of the Treaty of Versailles, they were **shocked!** There was an outcry against it. Newspapers ran campaigns against it and vowed Germany would seek revenge. There were protest marches.

- **The Germans did not feel they had started the war** but they nonetheless had to sign the treaty that said they were to blame.
- **Many did not even feel they had lost the war.** They believed the Weimar Republic was to blame for their defeat and that the army generals had been **stabbed in the back** by the 'cowardly' politicians stopping the war by signing the treaty.
- **Germans hated having to pay reparations** – the country was already bankrupt and many people were starving.
- **The loss of German territories caused a loss of pride in their country.** Some Germans would now be living in 'foreign' countries.
- **Germans resented losing so much of their army, navy and air forces.** It was unfair. No other country had been disarmed.

Opponents of the Weimar Republic **blamed the new government** for signing the Treaty of Versailles.

Key terms

Colonies – countries or areas of land occupied and ruled by another country

Reparations – compensation for the damage caused by the First World War demanded by the victorious Allies from Germany on the grounds that Germany was to blame for the war

Revision task

Create your own memory map showing 'Problems faced by the Weimar Republic 1918–23'. As you revise pages 102–106, add branches for:

- **Defeat in the First World War**
- **Treaty of Versailles**
- **Political violence**
- **Invasion of the Ruhr**
- **Hyper-inflation**

Why was the Republic so unpopular with many Germans?

Revised

Reason 1: The impact of the Treaty of Versailles

You saw how the Germans felt on page 103. Even the moderates who supported the Weimar government still thought that the Treaty of Versailles humiliated and weakened Germany. They blamed the government for everything that resulted from it. Remember LAMB!

Reason 2: The Weimar Constitution

A **constitution** is the set of rules that says how a country is governed. After 50 years of being ruled by the Kaiser (without democracy) the new constitution made the Weimar Republic one of the most democratic countries in the world!

- The **President** would be democratically elected.
- Members of the Reichstag were elected through the system of **proportional representation (PR)**.
- The President then chose a Chancellor from the Reichstag.
- The Chancellor ran the country day to day and **any new laws were voted on by the Reichstag** – to pass, a new law needed more than 50 per cent of the votes.
- **All men and women over the age of twenty could vote** by secret ballot to elect the members of the Reichstag. All adults had equal rights and the right of free speech.

Most Germans wanted this to succeed. However others were worried that democracy would lead to weak government. And **a small minority were totally opposed** to the new Republic. Left-wing and right-wing extremists tried to seize power to rule Germany their way.

Examiner's tip

The constitution gave the Republic structural weaknesses that would later prove very important.

- Article 48 gave the President 'rule by decree'. In the 1930s the Republic actually relied on this to get anything done!
- PR resulted in many smaller parties having seats in the Reichstag and chaotic coalition governments.
- All the judges and officials came from the Kaiser's time and hated the Republic.

Key terms

Reichstag – German Parliament

Proportional representation – the number of representatives from a given party is determined by the share or proportion of votes that party gains nationally **(PR)**

Chancellor – like the Prime Minister in Britain

Putsch – a sudden armed uprising, a political revolt

Extreme left-wing parties	Extreme right-wing parties
THE SPARTACIST LEAGUE were a Communist group who wanted a revolution. They did not trust government and didn't think it would improve workers' lives.	**THE FREIKORPS** were anti-communist, nationalist ex-soldiers. They helped the army against communist uprisings.
January 1919: THE SPARTACIST REVOLT They tried to turn workers' protests into a revolution, but they didn't have enough support. The German army and the Freikorps stopped the uprising and 100 workers were killed.	**1920: THE KAPP PUTSCH** The government disbanded the Freikorps. Led by Wolfgang Kapp, 12,000 Freikorps marched to Berlin to overthrow the government. They got in, but Berlin workers protested against them and stopped work which made it impossible to rule, so Kapp fled after four days and the government returned to power.
THE COMMUNIST PARTY were German workers who were angry about bad pay and conditions and who wanted more rights.	**THE NAZI PARTY** were led by Adolf Hitler. They believed democratic government was weak, and wanted one political party and leader.
1920: THE RED RISING IN THE RUHR A communist 'Red Army' of 50,000 workers occupied the Ruhr and took control of raw materials. The Germany army and the Freikorps stopped the uprising and 1000 workers were killed.	**1923: THE MUNICH PUTSCH** The Nazis burst into a meeting and forced the leader of Bavaria (Kahr) to support their plan to seize power, but next day he withdrew his support. The German army defeated the Nazis easily. Hitler was sent to jail.

The invasion of the Ruhr, 1923

Germany was struggling to pay reparations, and did not pay anything in 1922. Ebert tried to negotiate a reduction but the French insisted that Germany must pay, and then **invaded the Ruhr** in January 1923 to take what was owed to them in the form of raw materials and goods. The French seized mines, factories and railways. This was quite legal under the terms of the Treaty of Versailles!

In response, the German government told their workers to go on strike using 'passive resistance' as a protest against the invasion. The government still paid the workers, which cost them a lot of money since no money was coming in from selling goods or raw materials in the Ruhr. This helped lead to **hyper-inflation**.

Hyper-inflation, 1923

WELCOME TO A GERMAN ECONOMICS LESSON!

Do not worry about the details of hyper-inflation – you really just need to understand the basics:

1. The German government runs out of money.

2. It prints more money to pay workers and repay its debts.

3. People don't trust the money so the only sensible thing to do is to spend it quickly!

4. Shops and suppliers put up prices – this means that people have to be paid more and so the government needs even more money, and so on, in a vicious circle.

5. Prices rise at an incredible rate: in 1919 a stamp costs about 1 mark. In 1923 a stamp costs about 22 million marks!

Impact of hyper-inflation

These are many examples of the impact of hyper-inflation. Some are quit amusing. Others are very sad.

- Wages were taken home in wheel barrows!
- People used bank notes to light fires and gave them to children to play with.
- One woman left a basket full of bank notes outside a shop – thieves stole the basket and left the money.
- Farmers did not want to sell their food for worthless money and so there were major food shortages.
- Some people died from starvation and others turned to crime.
- One of the most damaging long-term impacts for the Weimar Republic was that people who had been saving carefully for years saw their savings become worthless.
- However, people in debt gained because their loans were worth much less than they had been.

Examiner's tip

Remember how this topic overlaps with Topic 3.2.

- Hyper-inflation led to political violence and riots. There were rebellions in Berlin and the Rhineland.
- Then in November 1923 Hitler and the Nazis staged their Munich Putsch.

How far did life improve for German people between 1924 and 1929?

In 1923, **Stresemann** became Chancellor of Germany. During his time as Chancellor and then as Foreign Minister, he tried to solve the problems that faced the Weimar Republic.

Examiner's tip

One popular angle for exam questions is whether Stresemann's reforms rebuilt Germany or whether he just 'papered over the cracks'. This table will help you to prepare for such a question.

Problem	Stresemann's solutions	However ...
Hyper-inflation	Stresemann introduced a **new currency**, the Rentenmark. This was accepted by the German people and **inflation was brought under control**.	People who had **savings** did not get them back and blamed the Weimar Republic.
Invasion of the Ruhr	Stresemann called off passive resistance in the Ruhr. He **promised to pay reparations**, so the French left the Ruhr. Industries restarted production.	Some Germans thought this was **weak** and that Stresemann had given in to the French.
Germany was not trusted by other countries	Stresemann signed the **Locarno Pact** with Britain, France and Belgium in 1925. They all promised not to invade each other. Germany accepted that it could not get back land taken away by the Treaty of Versailles (Stresemann won the Nobel Peace Prize) The **League of Nations** gave Germany 'Great Power' status, so it got a say in major decisions.	Some Germans thought it was **weak** to agree not to try to invade other countries where they had once had land. Again this was seen as giving in to the French.
Reparations to pay	Stresemann promised to pay reparations. The **Dawes Plan** (1924) reorganised the reparations so that Germany had longer to pay them. The **Young Plan** (1929) cut them to £31,000 million.	**Many Germans did not think that any reparations should be paid at all**. The repayment extension meant that Germans could be in debt until the 1980s!
Need to rebuild German economy	Stresemann asked the rich USA for **loans.** He used them to rebuild Germany. Many US firms set up factories in Germany. Stresemann's government set up labour exchanges and unemployment pay, and built 3 million new homes. These all helped the poor and unemployed.	The economy was **dependent** on the USA. Wages did not rise for all workers; farmers lost out. Unemployment was still high. Rich people had to pay higher taxes.
Political stability	Stresemann formed a coalition with other moderate parties so the Reichstag could govern more effectively.	The coalition depended on Stresemann. What would happen if he died?

Revision task

Go back to your mind map of problems facing Weimar Germany and add a new set of 'Recovery?' branches round the outside to summarise how far you think each problem had been solved.

Examiner's tip

The big idea is that the right-wing nationalist groups did not trust the Weimar government, even when things seemed to be improving. They looked for ways to undermine it.

What were the achievements of the Weimar period?

After the chaos of 1919–23, just to have survived at all was quite an achievement! But what else?

- **The Constitution** was a real attempt to create a **new democratic republic** that represented everyone. **Proportional representation** meant that parties got seats based on how many votes they got. **All Germans had equal rights**.
- Gradually **Stresemann rebuilt the German economy.** Industry in Germany was at pre-war levels by 1928. Wages rose.
- **Culture flourished** with lots of new ideas and approaches.

	What was new?	Individuals	However…
Art	• Weimar art tried to show everyday life. • Corrupt rich people were painted in an angry and distorted way. • Bauhaus College in Dessau became a centre for European artists like Kandinsky to go to teach.	George Grosz – painted distorted images of corrupt men. Otto Dix – a famous Weimar artist.	This was mainly centred in Berlin; other parts of Germany were not affected, were not interested or did not approve. Some thought they represented a **moral decline**. Some disapproved still more because these cultural changes were led by American immigrants or **Jews**. The **Wandervogel movement** was a reaction to the new developments. They wanted a return to simple country values.
Cinema	• A Golden Age for German cinema. • Science fiction and horror films were produced using techniques still used today.	Fritz Lang – directed *Nosferatu*, the first vampire horror movie. Marlene Dietrich – famous film star.	
Architecture	• The *Bauhaus* group of artists and designers produced work that used new technology, basic shapes and colours and was economical, using new materials like concrete with glass and steel.	Walter Gropius – famous architect.	
Theatre	• Theatre and opera portrayed the time. Plays were set in the 1920s. Arias were sung in bath tubs. The aim was to bring theatre to working people.	Bertolt Brecht – director and producer.	
Cabaret	• Berlin was famous for its liberated nightlife with naked dancers. Sex was discussed openly and sung about. Homosexuality was no longer frowned upon.		

Exam practice

1. Briefly describe how the Treaty of Versailles restricted German power. **[5]**

2. Explain why the Weimar Republic had serious problems in the period 1919 to 1923. **[7]**

3. 'The Weimar Republic was in a healthy state by 1929.' How far do you agree with this statement? **[9]**

Answers online

3.2 How was Hitler able to come to power in Germany?

You have already revised (page 103) the four groups who tried to overthrow the Weimar Republic. One of these groups was **the Nazi Party, led by Adolf Hitler**. They were easily crushed at the Munich Putsch but after that failure they changed their tactics, decided to seek election rather than taking over by force. And to many people's surprise by 1933 the Nazis were the most popular political party in Germany and Hitler became Chancellor.

There were many different factors that helped the Nazis to power but the most important was the worldwide economic depression which crippled the German economy in the early 1930s.

HITLER'S RISE TO POWER	
1889	Born in Austria.
1907	Moves to Vienna and fails to get a place in art school.
1914–18	Joins the German army and fights in the First World War.
1919	Sent by army to spy on German Workers' Party. Agrees with their ideas and joins the party.
1920	Helps to establish core beliefs and political views of the party and renames it National Socialist German Workers' Party (or Nazi Party). He creates its swastika emblem.
1921	Becomes leader of the Nazi Party, and his popularity grows. **He is a charismatic speaker and inspires others**. He sets up the SA – the Nazi Party's private army.
1922	Nazi Party grows to 20,000 members.
1922	Sets up the Hitler Youth, which provides activities for young people and spreads Nazi ideas.
1923	**The Munich Putsch:** Nazi Party now has 55,000 members. They believe the democratic government is weak and so decide to take over the government. The putsch fails and Hitler is sent to prison but he gains **huge publicity** and serves only nine months because right-wing judges sympathise with his views.
1924	Writes *Mein Kampf* ('My Struggle') while in prison, outlining his main ideas about how Germany should be ruled. He forces a change of tactics for the Nazi Party.
1924	Nazi candidates enter Reichstag elections for the first time. They win 24 seats.
1925	Sets up the SS, a fanatical, loyal, personal bodyguard.
1925	*Mein Kampf* published. It becomes a best seller.
1928	Nazis win just 12 seats in the Reichstag elections.
1929	The Wall Street crash leads to…
1930–33	A worldwide economic depression and high unemployment in Germany.
1932	**July elections:** Nazis win 207 seats and become largest party, but Hitler is not invited to become Chancellor.
1932	**Nov elections:** Nazis win 196 seats. Nazis still the largest party but Hitler still not invited to become Chancellor.
1933	**Jan:** None of the other possible Chancellors has support in the Reichstag so reluctantly President Hindenberg makes Hitler Chancellor.

Key issues

- What did the Nazi Party stand for in the 1920s?
- Why were the Nazis unsuccessful before 1929?
- Why were the Nazis successful after 1929?
- Who supported the Nazis, and why?
- How important was Hitler in the success of the Nazis?

What did the Nazi Party stand for in the 1920s?

Revised

In 1920, the Nazi Party had the following political aims and beliefs:

- To **end the Treaty of Versailles** and ignore its terms.
- To **refuse to pay reparations**.
- To **take over land in Eastern Europe** to make space for the growing German population.
- To **provide pensions** for old people, and **help for small businesses**.
- That, other than income from work, there should be **no other incomes allowed**.
- That **criminals should be punished by death**.
- That **no new non-Germans should be allowed** to come to live in Germany.
- That **only those with German blood** should be members of the German **country (no Jews)**.
- That in school, **pupils should learn to love their country** and **physical fitness** was vital.

In *Mein Kampf* in 1924, Hitler added the following aims and beliefs:

- To **smash communism** (which stood up for the rights of the workers) and to destroy Russia (which was a communist state).
- To **rebuild the army**.
- To **invade land in Eastern Europe**.
- To **unite all German-speaking people** in one country.
- That **there should be one strong leader** – no debates and no majority decisions as this makes government weak.
- That **Aryans are the master race**. All other races (especially the Jews) are inferior.

The Munich Putsch

It was a failure in the short term.

- It was a direct response to the chaos of the Ruhr invasion and hyper-inflation (see page 104).
- Hitler and 600 SA members interrupted a political meeting in a beer hall, forced the speaker von Kahr (an ex-general) to join them, then…
- The next day they 'marched' on Munich. The army stopped them; 16 were killed. Hitler and the leaders were arrested.

However, in the longer term it was a success for the Nazis:

- The trial gave Hitler **huge publicity**.
- While in prison he wrote his best-seller *Mein Kampf*.
- He got off with a light sentence because right-wing judges sympathised with his views.
- He forced the change of tactics.

> **Revision task**
>
> Create a memory map to show the main aims and beliefs of the Nazi Party. Use colour and drawings to illustrate your points. You could group them into four branches:
>
> - nationalism;
> - socialism;
> - racism; and
> - anti-Communism.

> **Key term**
>
> **Aryan** – Nazi term for a white European of pure stock, blond-haired, blue-eyed and physically fit. In practice, it became used as the Nazi term for non-Jewish Germans

> **Examiner's tip**
>
> Hitler's light sentence is a good example of the way that officials who were supposed to support the Weimar Republic did not really do so.

Why were the Nazis unsuccessful before 1929?

Revised

After the failure of the Munich Putsch of 1923, the Nazis realised that they could not take over by force. Instead, they had to be voted into government by the German people. They focused on running public meetings and recruiting new members.

However, in the elections of 1928, the Nazi Party gained only 3 per cent of the vote. Many German people did not want to vote for the Nazi Party then for the following reasons:

- **Peace and prosperity** – Stresemann's policies had overcome the problems of the early 1920s, Germany was at peace with other countries and the economy was doing well. Many factory workers were better off than they had been before.
- **Lack of support from workers** – If factory workers wanted change in the government, they tended to support the Communist Party rather than the Nazis.
- **The Nazis frightened people** – The SA were seen as very violent and Nazi ideas were anti-Semitic.

The only groups that the Nazis succeeded with were the **farmers** and the **middle classes**, who both liked the Nazi anti-Communist message.

Examiner's tip

During the prosperous years 1924–28, the Nazi views were seen as extreme or even irrelevant by most Germans – a relic of the troubled and violent post-war years of 1919–23.

Why were the Nazis successful after 1929?

Revised

From 1929 onwards the Nazi fortunes improved dramatically.

- In the 1930 election the Nazis had their first breakthrough. They won 18 per cent of the vote and got 107 seats in the Reichstag.
- In July 1932 they won 37 per cent of the vote and 207 seats. They were now the largest party. They did not have an overall majority so Hitler did not become Chancellor – yet (you will find out how that happened on the next page).

This was a remarkable turnaround for a party that did so badly in 1928 and it needs explaining.

Revision task

This is a favourite topic for exam questions so make sure you know these factors well and know how they contributed to Nazi success. Create a revision card for each factor. On one side write the heading, on the other key points. Include a card for 'political deal'. If you can add examples to each card from your course even better.

Effects of the Wall Street Crash and the Great Depression

The German economy was dependent on loans from America. In 1929, the American stock market, known as 'Wall Street', crashed. It led to a worldwide economic collapse and the period of history known as the Great Depression. This soon affected Germany.

- US banks started to **recall their loans.** German companies were unable to pay.
- Many German firms went **bankrupt**. Millions lost their jobs.
- With more unemployment came **less demand** for food and goods, sinking Germany deeper into depression.
- By 1932, **unemployment** in Germany had **reached 6 million**.

The Weimar government appeared to stumble aimlessly through this crisis, not knowing what to do. The government were scared of a repeat of the hyper-inflation of 1923, so did not want to spend money they did not have on solving unemployment.

This helped the Nazi Party because…

The German people blamed the Weimar Republic for the Great Depression and for high unemployment, and became less supportive as unemployment and poverty grew. They started to turn to more extremist political parties, such as the Nazis.

Nazi promises

Hitler and the Nazis promised to:

- solve the economic crisis and get people back to work
- destroy the Treaty of Versailles
- restore the power of the army
- make Germany powerful again
- be strong leaders of the country.

This helped the Nazi Party because…

These were almost exactly the same things they had been saying in the 1920s. The difference was that the chaos and despair of the depression years meant that many ordinary Germans had lost faith in democratic political parties. German people now wanted to hear these messages.

Fear of communism

As their lives became more difficult, more workers started to support the Communist Party. However, this terrified many of the German businessmen and farmers, because they had seen communism in action in the Soviet Union where the government had taken over the land and wealth from big industries and farmers.

The middle class, the businessmen and the farmers didn't want the Communist Party to get into power, so they turned to the Nazis because of their anti-communist stance. Rich businessmen gave them money for campaigning.

Hitler's leadership

Hitler was a charismatic and influential public speaker who was able to get across Nazi ideas and make the German people believe what he was saying. He was also surrounded by a team of very loyal and effective leaders.

Hitler's speeches gained a great deal of support for the Nazis.

Nazi propaganda

- Josef Goebbels was in charge of Nazi propaganda. He used the **latest technology** – film, loudspeakers and slide shows.
- In 1932, Hitler **travelled around Germany by plane** so that he could talk to as many people as possible.
- **Mass rallies** made people feel proud to be German and added a sense of order and discipline.
- **Posters** were used effectively to spread Nazi ideas.

This propaganda got the Nazi message across to people very effectively. It increased support for the Nazis.

Local organisations

By 1929, the Nazis had well over 100,000 members, and local parties all over Germany. They were well organised.

- Local leaders ran **public meetings**. The Nazi party provided carefully trained speakers.
- Local parties **helped the unemployed** by providing soup kitchens and shelters or recruiting them into the local SA.
- The **Hitler Youth** (see page 120) from 1922 provided activities.
- The SA even gained a reputation for being **disciplined young men** (not the threatening thugs of the 1920s).

At a time when the national government seemed incompetent or ineffective these local measures impressed many ordinary Germans and increased support for the Nazis. The apparent discipline of the SA was attractive when there was so much violence around the election meetings of 1930 and 1932 – even though the SA often stirred up the violence in the first place!

Weak opposition

There were two natural opponents to the Nazis: the Social Democrats (who were the largest party) and the Communists.

- Neither party took the Nazis seriously and were more concerned with battling each other.
- Voters did not trust the Social Democrats (the ruling party) because they didn't seem to know what to do.

Weak opposition meant that the Nazis' policies were not challenged or questioned. The opposition offered nothing new while the Nazis did.

Political problems

- The most successful Weimar politician of the 1920s, Stresemann, died of a stroke in 1929, just days before the Wall Street Crash.
- The democratic ideals of the Weimar constitution caused problems. No party had a majority and there was a series of weak, short-lived governments.
- Some of the measures taken by the government actually made the Depression worse. For example they cut pay and benefits for government employees, leading to poverty.
- Because of the weak government, President Hindenberg used Article 48 of the constitution to rule by decree (without getting laws approved by the Reichstag).

The weak government made the Nazi message of strong government more attractive. In fact some people say that Hindenberg's ruling by decree had ended democracy in the Weimar Republic already. And remember some people had never forgiven the Weimar government for the Treaty of Versailles, the 'stab in the back', reparations and hyper-inflation.

The political deal

Following the June 1932 elections, the Nazis were the largest party in the Reichstag, but they did not have an overall majority. No other party wanted to work with them. President Hindenburg had to appoint a Chancellor. He did not want Hitler so he appointed his friend von Papen. But the Reichstag did not support von Papen!

So the result was **stalemate,** and another election in November 1932. The Nazis lost seats but were still the biggest party. This time Hitler did a deal with von Papen, who persuaded Hindenberg to appoint Hitler as Chancellor and himself as Vice Chancellor. Von Papen thought he could control Hitler. How wrong he was!

Who supported the Nazis, and why?

Many Germans changed their minds and supported the Nazis for the first time in the 1932 election. For example:

People who had lost their jobs in the factories because of the Great Depression believed the promises that the Nazis would improve the economy. When they were unemployed, the government had not done anything to help them, while the Nazis had run soup kitchens and shelters for the homeless.

Small businessmen whose businesses were struggling because of the Great Depression believed that the Nazis would improve the economy so that people would spend more money on goods and their profits would improve.

Industrialists (big business) and **bankers** welcomed the Nazis' anti-Communist message and they wanted to weaken the trade unions.

Farmers – as food prices had dropped and the Great Depression meant people could afford less food, small farms went bankrupt. Improving the economy would improve the farming industry as people would be able to buy more food.

People who wanted a strong leader – people were fed up of the different parties within the democratic government arguing over what they should do. They wanted someone to take charge of the country to sort it out.

People who were scared – there was a lot of violence on the streets and the Nazi army, the SA, gave the promise of law and order.

How important was Hitler in the success of the Nazis?

It should be clear from the past few pages that Hitler was not the only reason the Nazis came to power in 1932. The Nazi success was a combination of

- factors beyond Nazi control (such as the Wall Street Crash, or weakness of the opposition) and
- factors within their control (such as propaganda or local organisation).

You already have a list on your revision cards.

But where does Hitler fit into this? How important was he?

- He was a **charismatic leader**. He knew how to motivate people and his supporters were very loyal to him right to the end.
- He was a **talented public speaker** who could stir a crowd into a frenzy and could communicate Nazi ideas very simply. This was vital in a time when public meetings and rallies were a main form of communication (as important as television or the internet is to a modern politician).
- He was a good **organiser**.
- He **directed Nazi policy**. Nazi policies were his policies.
- He became the **focus for much of the Nazi propaganda**. If you compare Nazi election posters from 1928 and 1932 you can see how Hitler became the focus. Hitler was presented as:
  - a war hero and a loyal German
  - someone who understood ordinary Germans
  - someone with the desire to make Germany great again.

Sort the following into
  a) factors that the Nazis controlled
  b) factors that were beyond Nazi control

- Fear of communism
- Hitler's speaking skills
- The political deal with von Papen and Hindenberg
- Nazi election posters
- Unstable and weak government
- The Wall Street Crash
- Nazi propaganda
- Unemployment
- Nazi soup kitchens for the unemployed
- Weak opposition

Which list do you think is more significant in explaining the Nazi success? It may not be the longer list. You might think that one or two items bear much more weight than others.

Examiner's tip

For advice about usefulness (Question 1) see page 47. Consider the ways in which this helps you understand Nazi tactics and messages. Also consider what else you need to know to really understand the success.

For 'describe' and 'explain' questions such as 2 and 3 refer to the advice on pages 5–6.

Examiner's tip

Question 4 is an iceberg question. It mentions one factor but in order to answer you need to consider the other factors too (see page 13). Use your revision cards. You could structure your answer like this:

- How the depression helped Hitler and the Nazis.
- What other factors helped the Nazis. You don't have to consider them all but mention at least three.
- A conclusion in which you answer the question.

Exam practice

1. Study Source A. How useful is this source for explaining Nazi success in the elections of 1932? **[7]**

Source A: *A Nazi election poster of 1932. The text reads: 'Women! Millions of men without work. Millions of children without a future. Save the German family. Vote Adolf Hitler!'*

2. Briefly describe how the 1929 Wall Street Crash led to problems in Germany. **[5]**
3. Explain why the Nazis had little success in elections before 1928. **[7]**
4. Was the depression in Germany the most important reason why Hitler was able to come to power by the beginning of 1933? **[8]**

Answers online

3.3 The Nazi regime: How effectively did the Nazis control Germany, 1933–1945?

Ten steps from Chancellor to Führer	
January 1933	**1 Hitler becomes Chancellor** He is leader of Germany but his power is limited. He can only pass laws if the Reichstag agree and he does not have a majority in the Reichstag.
27 February	**2 The Reichstag fire** The Reichstag building in Berlin was set on fire by a communist, Marinus van der Lubbe. The Nazis claimed this was a communist plot to take over Germany. Communist leaders around Germany were arrested. Hindenberg gave Hitler emergency powers to imprison people without trial to stop the communist plot. Hitler used this power to arrest people who opposed the Nazi party. The Reichstag fire was such a gift to the Nazis that many people believe the Nazis set it up. There is no conclusive proof but there is no doubt they used it decisively.
5 March	**3 March 1933 elections** Hitler used the fear of communism to campaign in the elections and the Nazis' anti-communist message was spread through propaganda. Nazis arrested the 81 communist members of the Reichstag. The Nazis achieved 52 per cent of the vote.
24 March	**4 The Enabling Act** Hitler wanted to pass laws without having to consult the Reichstag or the President. He needed to get 66 per cent of votes from the Reichstag to get this Act passed. The Communist Party were expelled from the Reichstag and couldn't vote. The Centre Party were persuaded to vote for the Act by Hitler's promises to protect the Catholic Church. Only the Social Democrats voted against it. This led to 82 per cent of the Reichstag voting for the Act (441 votes to 94).
2 May	**5 Trade unions were disbanded** The Enabling Act was used to arrest trade union leaders and merge trade unions into the German Labour Front (DAF), which was an organisation controlled by the Nazis.
July	**6 Other political parties were banned** The Enabling Act meant there was a ban on forming new political parties. The Communist Party and the Social Democratic Party had already been banned. Only one party was allowed in Germany – the Nazi Party.
July	**7 Concordat with the Catholic Church** This agreement between state and church meant that church rights would be protected but the Catholic Church was banned from political activity.
29–30 June 1934	**8 The Night of the Long Knives** There was a power struggle brewing between the SA and the army. The SA had been set up by Hitler in 1921 to protect Nazi meetings (see page 105). Ernst Röhm was its leader. He was a close friend of Hitler, but he was very powerful and a potential rival. The SA, with 3 million members, had grown bigger than the German army and wanted to control it. Hitler wanted to support the army, expand it, and buy new weapons. The army feared being taken over by the SA. On the Night of the Long Knives, SA leaders were taken from their homes in the middle of the night and shot. Up to 400 people were killed. Röhm was arrested and imprisoned. When he refused to commit suicide, he was shot. This showed the rest of Germany how ruthless Hitler was in his pursuit of power.
2 August	**9 Hitler becomes Führer** President Hindenberg died and Hitler made himself President as well as Chancellor. He called himself Führer (Supreme Leader).
August	**10 Army oath** The government army took an oath of loyalty to Hitler. All soldiers vowed to obey him and give their lives for him.

> **Revision task**
>
> The information on this page is important to learn. Make your own version of the timeline summarising Hitler's ten steps to power. Use drawings and colours to make it easier to remember. Add a sentence to explain how each step helped Hitler.

The Weimar Republic and democracy had been destroyed and Germany was now a dictatorship.

Key issues

- How much opposition was there and how effectively did the Nazis deal with it?
- How did the Nazis use culture and the mass media to control the people?
- Why did the Nazis persecute many groups in German society?
- Was Nazi Germany a totalitarian state?

How much opposition was there and how effectively did the Nazis deal with it?

Revised

Once in power, Hitler banned all other political parties so there was no official opposition inside or outside the Reichstag. People who opposed the Nazis were jailed. All official bodies were 'Nazified'.

Key term

SS – short for Schutzstaffel (protection squad). Originally the private bodyguard for Hitler and other Nazi leaders, the SS later became the main instrument of terror in Nazi Germany

How was opposition dealt with?

The SS (led by Himmler)

- Originally Hitler's own bodyguard, built up to 240,000 members.
- All recruits had to be blond, blue-eyed (Aryan) and fit.
- They had the power to arrest people without trial and search houses.

The Gestapo (led by Heydrich)

- The state **secret police** who could tap telephones, open mail and collect information from informers.
- Informers reported on local people who they believed were anti-Nazi.

Local wardens

- The country was divided into 42 'gaus', each with a Nazi **Gauleiter**, loyal to Hitler.
- Each town was divided into blocks, each with a **block leader**.
- Local wardens would visit these blocks to collect donations for the Nazi Party and to check support for the Nazis.
- Wardens reported to the Gestapo: their report could decide if a person got a job or if they were arrested for being anti-Nazi.

Concentration camps

- In the early days these were simply improvised camps, for example in disused factories. Opponents were taken there for short periods of questioning, torture and hard labour, and taught Nazi ideals.
- By the late 1930s, concentration camps were specially constructed camps in remote areas. They were run by a section of the SS called Death's Head Units.
- Jews, communists and anyone who criticised the Nazis went to these camps.

Police and courts

- The police were put under control of Himmler.
- Courts were under control of the Nazis, and Nazis were appointed as judges in 'People's Courts'.
- The number of crimes carrying the death penalty went up, including telling an anti-Nazi joke, or listening to foreign radio stations (including the BBC).

Revision task

On the next two pages are examples of opposition groups in Nazi Germany. There were similarities and differences between them. Make a table to compare them with these headings.

Name	Who?	When?	What were their aims?	What methods did they use?	How effective was Nazi control? (your mark out of 10 with a reason)

Former political opponents 1933–45

Who? Leaders and supporters of former opposition parties, including the Socialist Party, the Communist Party and the trade unions.

Aims? Democracy to be restored to Germany, with free speech and workers' rights.

Methods? Secret meetings, anti-Nazi graffiti slogans on walls, leaflets, strikes.

How effectively did the Nazis deal with them?
All opposition parties and trade unions were banned by July 1933. Thousands of the leaders and supporters were arrested and put into concentration camps. Others were tortured, beaten up or killed to scare people into supporting the Nazi Party. Those who didn't were forced into exile abroad or went into hiding to wait until democracy returned to Germany.

Edelweiss Pirates 1938–44

Who? Young working-class people. It was not a united organisation, just local groups.

Aims? To have fun and avoid Hitler Youth events.

Methods? Sang anti-Hitler songs, drank alcohol, had sex, wore badges with the edelweiss flower or skull and crossbones. Some of the groups attacked Nazi officials. During the war, some sheltered communists and army deserters.

How effectively did the Nazis deal with them?
In 1944, one group killed a Nazi youth leader in Cologne, and some Edelweiss Pirates were hanged. But the Nazis could not control this opposition as it was not a united organisation.

The White Rose Group 1942–43

Who? A small group of students at Munich University, led by Sophie and Hans Scholl.

Aims? To shame Germans into protesting about the Nazis, and to urge them to overthrow Hitler. Sophie wrote, 'Germany's name will be disgraced forever unless the German youth finally rises up'.

Methods? Spread anti-Nazi messages by handing out leaflets and writing graffiti.

How effectively did the Nazis deal with them?
Sophie and Hans were arrested, tortured and executed and the group disbanded.

The Churches 1933–45

Who? Ninety per cent of the population belonged to either the Roman Catholic Church (22 million people) or the Protestant Church (40 million people). They were by far the biggest non-Nazi organisation left in Germany after 1933.

Aims? Some Church leaders actively supported the Nazis, while others actively opposed them. Many did neither and wanted to keep religion and politics separate.

Methods? Mostly they carried on with their normal activities: services, youth groups, schools. Some got involved in political opposition. Bishop von Galen of Münster opposed euthanasia of the mentally ill. Hitler agreed and stopped it. Martin Niemöller set up the 'Confessional Church' to oppose Nazism. He was sent to a concentration camp in 1938.

How effectively did the Nazis deal with them?
However much he wanted to, Hitler did not dare shut down the Churches because they had so much support from the German people.

- He made a deal ('concordat') with the **Roman Catholic** Church – if Hitler would leave their members alone, they would not get involved with politics.
- The Nazis wanted to control the **Protestant Church** by turning it into the **Reich Church**. Reich Church pastors had to take an oath of loyalty to Hitler. Those who resisted, such as Martin Niemöller, were sent to a concentration camp.
- In 1936, Hitler stopped all Church youth groups (young people now had to join the Hitler Youth) and, by 1939, he had closed down nearly all Church schools so that he could control the minds of the youth.

Many pastors did not take the oath of loyalty, and formed the non-Nazi Confessional Church. However, there wasn't a lot of opposition from the Church. Only about 50 pastors out of 17,000 were arrested for activities opposing the Nazis.

Army officers – the July bomb plot 1944

Who? A group of upper-class army officers (the 'Beck Group') disgusted by Hitler's actions – especially SS brutality during the invasion of the USSR (see page 126).

Aims? To assassinate Hitler and take over. They were aware that Germany was losing the Second World War and wanted to end Hitler's interference in military strategy.

Methods? There had been earlier plots to assassinate Hitler. This plot known as the 'July bomb plot' set out to blow up Hitler in his military headquarters.

How effectively did the Nazis deal with them? The July bomb plot plans failed – the bomb went off but Hitler was not killed. All his known opponents, whether or not they were part of that plan, were rounded up – 5000 people were arrested and executed.

(see page 126)

Examiner's tip

Although the Nazis managed to scare most people into obedience that does not mean that everyone agreed with them, as you can see from the five case studies here.

The case studies show two other important things:

a) Opposition was minor before 1939. Times were good and the penalties for opposition were extreme.

b) Some people who supported Hitler and the Nazis in the 1930s became opponents in later years particularly once the Second World War started going badly (for example the army officers).

Remember this when you come to examine the impact of war on life in Germany. Just because some knowledge is covered in one topic, it doesn't mean you can't use it to answer questions on a different topic.

Revision task

Other examples of wartime opposition are: Helmüth Hübener; the Bielski brothers; the Kreisau circle. Do some research of your own to find out what they did and what happened to them. It could improve your marks if you have your own examples.

Why wasn't there more opposition to the Nazi Party?

Self-interest: to get anywhere in Nazi Germany you had to be a Nazi Party member. Nazis got the best jobs, the best houses, special privileges. Businessmen joined to boost their businesses.	**Terror:** People were scared to oppose the Nazis because they didn't want to be killed or put in a concentration camp. They were scared to tell anyone they didn't like the Nazis because potentially anyone could be an informer and report them to the Gestapo.	**Success:** Some people liked the Nazis – they had built up the army and navy, there was less unemployment and more order on the streets –better than the idea of a communist revolution.
Propaganda: The Nazis used propaganda effectively to persuade people they were doing great things.	**Fun:** The Nazis provided leisure activities for German workers: holidays, picnics, youth activities. They also provided entertaining films.	**No alternative:** There was no other political party to support; no organisations, leaders or meetings, as all were banned.

How did the Nazis use culture and the mass media to control the people?

Josef Goebbels was made Minister of Propaganda and National Enlightenment. He took control of all of the mass media. The main aim of propaganda was to give German people a Nazi view of events.

NEWSPAPERS

- All newspapers supported the Nazis – any that didn't were shut down.
- Each day, the Ministry of Propaganda told papers what stories to print, what angle the writers should take and what photos they could use.
- Newspapers were displayed in public places so everyone could read them.

BOOKS

- From 1933, the Reich Chamber of Culture organised official burnings of books written by communists, Jews or anyone the Nazis didn't approve of.
- They also burned books about any ideas the Nazis didn't approve of.

RADIO

- All radio broadcasting was controlled by the Nazis.
- Broadcasts were of Hitler's speeches, German history and German music.
- Cheap radios ('People's Receivers') were produced and loudspeakers were set up in public areas so lots of people could listen to the broadcasts.
- No foreign radio stations were allowed. Listening to them was punishable by death. Remember those block wardens (see page 115) – people could hear a radio!

FILMS

- Feature films were made in Germany and censored by Goebbels.
- Most were adventure stories, love stories or comedies.
- Before each feature there would be a newsreel made by Goebbels' film makers.
- One of the most famous propaganda films was 'Triumph of the Will' by Leni Riefenstahl about the 1934 Nuremberg rally.

RALLIES

- Presented an image of law and order and control.
- Hitler gave dramatic speeches.
- The stadium at Nuremberg was used effectively to create an image of unity.

ART AND ARCHITECTURE

- Public buildings were copies of the buildings of Greece and Rome.
- Private homes were 'country style'.
- Hitler had tried to be an artist – he hated the art of the Weimar Republic and preferred pictures which showed powerful German heroes and family scenes.

BERLIN OLYMPICS 1936

- This had been planned before the Nazis came to power.
- Goebbels saw the Olympics as a chance to showcase Nazi ideals and for foreigners to see what Hitler was capable of.
- The German team was professionally trained.
- Modern technology was used. TV coverage was new and used for the first time at a sporting event. Radio coverage was praised by foreign journalist. The most modern timing equipment was used.
- Germany won most medals.
- **BUT...** Black US athlete Jesse Owens and other black members of the US track and field team won thirteen medals. This challenged Nazi ideas that Aryans were a superior race.

Why did the Nazis persecute many groups in German society?

Revised ☐

Hitler wanted to build up Germany to make it a powerful country. The answer was to create the **Volk**, a super-race who were Aryan and physically and mentally fit. This would lead to Germany being a superpower in the world. Hitler intended to create the Volk by selective breeding – only allowing those with Aryan traits to be part of German society. He did this by rounding up the 'undesirables' who didn't fit the Nazi ideal, and getting rid of them.

> **Key term**
>
> **Volk** – people, in particular the German people

So the Nazis persecuted the following groups:

- **People who would not work** – criminals, tramps, beggars. They were rounded up and sent to concentration camps.

- **People who could not work** – the physically disabled and mental ill. They were put to death in gas chambers.

- **People who did not fit into 'normal' families** – this included homosexuals. They were arrested and sent to concentration camps. Many were castrated or used in medical experiments.

- **People who were not loyal to Hitler** – this included the socialists and the communists for political reasons and Jehovah's Witnesses for religious reasons. They were sent to concentration camps.

- **People who were not 'Aryans'** – this included black people, Jews and Gypsies.

  Jewish people suffered the worst persecution of all. This is covered on page 124.

  Gypsies were persecuted because they were not Aryan and did not do ordinary work. They were sent to concentration camps, and around 500,000 were later killed in the death camps.

Was Nazi Germany a totalitarian state?

Revised ☐

When the Nazis got into power in 1933 they did not just want to rule Germany, they wanted to **change** it. They wanted to win the hearts and minds of the German people. They wanted to create the Volksgemeinschaft, or the People's Community, in which everyone gave their all to Germany and put the needs of the state above their own.

A totalitarian state means a state in which every aspect of people's lives is controlled and monitored by those in power. The table below shows how Nazi Germany compared to a totalitarian state.

Features of a totalitarian state	Examples from Nazi Germany
Control of the media	• The Nazis controlled all aspects of the media. • There was strict **censorship** and therefore all news, information and rumour were controlled by the government.
Opposition is effectively controlled	• The Gestapo and SS controlled people's lives. • Informers were used and people did not oppose the Nazis due to fear of consequences.
People are expected to put the needs of the state above their own	• In the 1930s young people were trained up to serve the state as soldiers or mothers. • During 1939–45 they were forced to make many sacrifices for the war effort.
A supreme leader	• Hitler was a dictator. He did not need his laws approved by anyone. If he wanted something done the Nazi Party enforced it.

> **Exam practice**
>
> 1. Briefly describe the activities of the Gestapo and SS. **[5]**
>
> 2. Explain why the Enabling Act of March 1933 was so important in helping Hitler take control in Germany. **[7]**
>
> 3. 'The only way the Nazis controlled Germany was by terror.' How far do you agree with this statement? Explain your answer. **[8]**
>
> **Answers online**

3.4 The Nazi regime: What was it like to live in Nazi Germany?

The Nazis had a clear idea of what Germany should be like:

- racially pure – pure Aryans
- obedient people – putting Germany's needs above their own
- different roles for men and women – women as mothers, men as fighters.

The Nazis wanted to reshape every aspect of life in Germany to make this happen. So what life was like in Nazi Germany depended on:

- **Who you were**. If you fitted in with Nazi ideals then you were fine. If you did not then you suffered.
- **When you lived**. The 'peacetime' years of 1933–39 when the Nazis were rebuilding Germany were very different from the war years of 1939–45 when the Nazi state gradually unravelled.

Key issues

- How did young people react to the Nazi regime?
- How successful were Nazi policies towards women and the family?
- Did most people benefit from Nazi rule?
- How did the coming of war change life in Nazi Germany?

How did young people react to the Nazi regime?

Revised ☐

Hitler wanted to control the hearts and minds of young people in Germany, as he thought that if he could control young people, he could control the future. He did this through the Hitler Youth movement, and through German schools.

The Nazis wanted a Germany with traditional roles for women.

- Women would stay at home cooking and cleaning, and looking after babies.
- Men would go out to work, and fight in war if necessary.

The Hitler Youth and the school curriculum trained girls and boys for these roles.

Hitler Youth

Membership

- Founded in 1922, well before the Nazis took power.
- Membership compulsory in 1936.
- With Nazis in power, 80 per cent of young people were members.

Groups

- There were separate tiers for each age group and separate groups for girls and boys.

Revision task

Use the next five pages to create a memory map to show how different people (young people, women, workers, minorities) were affected by the policies of the Nazi Party. Try to use pictures or diagrams to show your thinking and include benefits and drawbacks for the different people.

Activities

- Swore an oath of loyalty to Hitler.
- Physical activities and listening to propaganda.
- Boys in the Hitler Youth (HJ) had to pass certain physical challenges and be ready to fight as a soldier. They wore uniforms, went on marches, did drill, and played 'war games'.
- Girls in the League of German Maidens (BDM) kept fit and were taught home-making (cooking, washing, sewing, looking after children).

Reaction of young people

- **Most young people** joined the Hitler Youth and many found that they enjoyed the activities that they took part in.
- By the end of the war much of the army was made up of young people from the Hitler Youth, who did not need to be trained as they had learned what they needed to do in the Hitler Youth.
- However, even when membership was compulsory, **some young people never joined in** and others who were forced to go hated it. They didn't like the long speeches and the repetitive physical activity.
- Some young people **rebelled** against Nazi ideas by joining the **Swing** Youth movement, where they could listen and dance to swing music – a blend of black jazz and white dance music, which the Nazis had banned. They wore English-style fashions, the girls wore make-up and the boys had long hair. During the war they met in 'swing clubs'. A common greeting was 'Heil Benny' after band leader Benny Goodman.

Examiner's tip

Both the Edelweiss Pirates and the White Rose Group (see page 116) date from the later years of the war and are good examples of how the war increased young people's opposition to the Nazi regime.

Schools

Teachers

- Ninety-seven per cent of all teachers were members of the Nazi Teacher's League.
- To progress as a teacher you had to be a Nazi.
- Women teachers were sacked.

Curriculum

- The whole curriculum was used to teach what Nazis wanted young people to think (indoctrination). Physical education was emphasised more than knowledge. In 1939, Hitler said 'I will have no intellectual training. Knowledge is ruin to my young men.' There were three double lessons of PE every week.
- Girls and boys were taught different skills, for example, boys learned to box while girls were taught home-making and childcare.
- Only German history was taught, starting from 1919 onwards. It was rewritten to support Nazi ideas – about how unfair the Treaty of Versailles was, and how wicked Jews and communists were.
- Teachers who refused to teach the curriculum were sacked.
- Even subjects such as maths had a Nazi twist, e.g. questions about calculating the cost of looking after the mentally ill.

Key term

Indoctrination – teaching people to accept ideas without question

Reaction of young people

There is very little evidence about what young people thought about school but just as the Hitler Youth suited some young people while others hated it, the same would be true of school.

How successful were Nazi policies towards women and the family?

The Nazi regime wanted families in Germany to be traditional, with a mother who stayed at home and had children, and a father who went out to work. They also had ideas about how women should dress and behave in public. The Nazis didn't like women to:

- wear high heels or trousers
- wear make-up
- have permed or dyed hair
- smoke.

Instead, they wanted women to wear simple clothes and no make-up. Here are some ways they forced or encouraged women to conform.

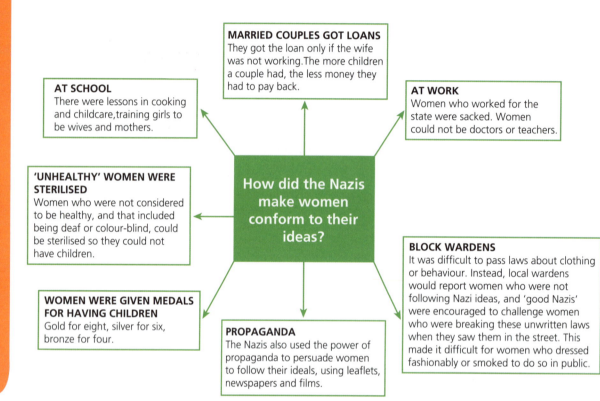

MARRIED COUPLES GOT LOANS
They got the loan only if the wife was not working. The more children a couple had, the less money they had to pay back.

AT SCHOOL
There were lessons in cooking and childcare, training girls to be wives and mothers.

AT WORK
Women who worked for the state were sacked. Women could not be doctors or teachers.

'UNHEALTHY' WOMEN WERE STERILISED
Women who were not considered to be healthy, and that included being deaf or colour-blind, could be sterilised so they could not have children.

How did the Nazis make women conform to their ideas?

BLOCK WARDENS
It was difficult to pass laws about clothing or behaviour. Instead, local wardens would report women who were not following Nazi ideas, and 'good Nazis' were encouraged to challenge women who were breaking these unwritten laws when they saw them in the street. This made it difficult for women who dressed fashionably or smoked to do so in public.

WOMEN WERE GIVEN MEDALS FOR HAVING CHILDREN
Gold for eight, silver for six, bronze for four.

PROPAGANDA
The Nazis also used the power of propaganda to persuade women to follow their ideals, using leaflets, newspapers and films.

How successful were these policies?

- Many women didn't want to give up their jobs, and the number of working women rose because the economy was doing very well.
- Many employers still wanted women to work in their factories as they were cheaper to employ than men.
- Nazi policies became particularly confused during the war – all women were called up to work, but they were also told, whether married or single, that they had to have four children!

Did most people benefit from Nazi rule?

Some gained, some lost. The big gainers were:

- **loyal Nazis** who got the best jobs and houses
- **workers** and **businessmen** who benefited from Nazi economic policies and reduced unemployment.

The Nazis were elected mainly because of Germany's economic problems. In 1933, unemployment was 5.5 million. By 1938 the Nazis had reduced this to 0.3 million by:

- **Building the armed forces:** In 1919, there were 100,000 people employed in the armed forces. The Nazis increased this to 1,400,000. All men aged 18–25 had to do two years' army service.
- **Re-arming Germany:** Rebuilding the armed forces meant that weapons and equipment were needed. Millions of jobs were created in factories that produced these. Iron, steel and coal production rose rapidly as a result, which benefited factory workers and owners.
- **An ambitious building programme:** Autobahns (motorways), schools, houses and hospitals were built by the government all over Germany.
- **Sacking communists and Jews:** Jews and opponents of the Nazis could not work and could not claim unemployment benefit. Women too were sacked because the Nazis wanted them to stay at home and be mothers.

Other economic policies were designed to:

- make Germany self-sufficient (e.g. by making oil from coal). This failed.
- encourage new industries such as electrics and medicines. There were some great successes such as jet engines and televisions.

> **Examiner's tip**
>
> A simple way to sum up 'control' in Nazi Germany is:
>
> - **the carrot** – to attract and reward people who conformed
> - **the stick** – to punish and terrorise people who opposed.
>
> Be sure to have at least two examples of each ready for the exam.

> **Examiner's tip**
>
> For the exam, you need to know what happened to people in Germany after Hitler came to power. Some people may have seen benefits in some aspects of their lives, but not in others. For example, a farmer's wife may have been happy about the benefits that Nazis gave to farmers, but if she had a hereditary condition she would have been sterilised. People in Germany do not just fall into one category.

Winners and losers

Benefits of Nazi economic policies	BUT...
Workers had the 'Strength Through Joy' movement, which provided people who worked hard and were loyal to Hitler with many perks, such as cinema tickets and family holidays. The Nazis organised better facilities in factories.	• Unions were banned. Instead workers had to join the DAF – the Nazi trade union. • Workers had no rights. Strikes were illegal and no one was allowed to leave their job without government permission. • Wages fell and working hours increased. • Workers were promised a Volkswagen car, for which they paid 5 marks a week in advance, but these were never delivered.
Farmers had supported the Nazi Party the most. Hitler supported farmers by guaranteeing food prices and offering them security if they fell behind on their rent.	• Farming stayed old-fashioned and inefficient. • The price of food rose, which hit factory workers hard because of their reduced wages.
Businessmen and factory owners did well out of the rebuilding of Germany. Workers were not allowed to strike, wages fell and working hours increased (thus profits went up). The government was spending money on goods made in factories.	**Small businesses** and small shops lost out in competition with big companies.

Persecution of minorities

Many groups were persecuted by the Nazis because they did not fit in with Nazi ideas. Look back to page 119. If you were any of the following in Nazi Germany:

- homeless or a beggar
- physically disabled or mentally ill
- homosexual
- socialist or communist
- Jehovah's Witness
- ethnic or religions minority such as black, Gypsy or Jewish

you might be persecuted, rounded up, imprisoned, sent to a concentration camp or killed. For many of those people life in Germany was a nightmare that they did not survive.

Nazi persecution of the Jews

Of all the minorities Jewish people suffered the worst treatment under Nazi rule.

Before the Nazis
Jews had suffered from religious prejudice for centuries but before the Nazis, Germany had been a tolerant place. Many Jews had moved to live in Germany to escape persecution in Russia in the late 1800s.

Up to 1933
Hitler and the Nazis put forward their **anti-Semitic** ideas. In *Mein Kampf*, Hitler blamed the Jews for Germany's problems. He blamed Jews for Germany's defeat in the First World War. Some Germans liked these Nazi views but many opposed them.

Nazis actively persecuted Jewish people even before the Nazis took power. The SA bullied and threatened Jewish shopkeepers. They organised boycotts of Jewish businesses.

1933–39
Once in power the Nazis' measures against the Jews became steadily more and more extreme.

Source A: *A poster for an anti-Semitic film, made by the Ministry of Propaganda, called* The Eternal Jew

> **Key term**
>
> **Anti-Semitic** – prejudiced against the Jews

Nazi persecution of Jews 1933–39	
1933	Jews were banned from certain jobs: they could not be judges, teachers, civil servants or lawyers.
1935	**Nuremberg Laws** – Jews could not be German citizens; Jews could not marry Aryans.
1936	Jews could not own typewriters, to prevent them from spreading their ideas in letters or articles.
1938	Jews were banned from being doctors, from running their own business, and from going to state schools, cinemas and swimming pools.
Nov 1938	**Kristallnacht** – In November 1938, a Jewish man shot a German diplomat in Paris. In retaliation, Nazi leaders encouraged their supporters to attack and smash up Jewish businesses, homes and synagogues. After two nights, 91 Jews had died. This was called Kristallnacht, 'the night of broken glass'. In the following months, 30,000 Jews were arrested and taken to concentration camps.
1939	Jews could not be nurses or dentists. There was a curfew – Jews had to be in their homes after nightfall. Jews had to hand over any jewellery, gold or silver to the police.

How did the coming of war change life in Nazi Germany?

Phase of the war	Effect on German people
September 1939–June 1941: War going well for Germany	
Germany had great **success** at the start of the war as they invaded Poland and France and most of Europe.	<ul><li>Germany was not self-sufficient. It could no longer import food from its neighbours so rationing was introduced from the start of the war. Germans had enough to eat but food was monotonous.</li><li>To save energy, hot water was also controlled.</li><li>There were some bombing raids on German cities – the first was on Berlin in 1940, but nothing as extreme as happened later in the war because the German defences were still strong.</li></ul>
June 1941–February 1943: Germany bogged down in war with Russia	
In June 1941 Hitler decided to invade the USSR (Russia). He had always said he intended to do this but it was a mistake and marked the start of a dramatic change in fortune for Germany. Instead of a quick victory Germany's best soldiers and equipment got **bogged down** in a long war with Russia that 'tore the heart out of the German army'.	<ul><li>**Bombing:** from 1942 air raids were more frequent and more ferocious. The Allies started their 'thousand bomber raids', dropping a combination of explosive and incendiary bombs.</li><li>There were **not enough doctors** to treat the wounded. Most were in the army, and Jews and women were not allowed to be doctors.</li><li>With so many people being killed in the war with the USSR, younger and less experienced **young men were drafted** into the army.</li><li>Because so many men were called up into the army, there was a **severe shortage of labour**. Employers wanted to bring in women to work, but this went against Nazi policy so workers were brought in from the countries that were occupied by Germany and used **as slave labour**.</li><li>With older teenagers working or fighting, **leadership of the Hitler Youth** was left to the younger teenagers – the Nazis had less control over the Hitler Youth.</li></ul>
February 1943–July 1944: Total War	
After defeat at the Battle of Stalingrad German forces **retreated** from Russia. The Nazis put every resource into stopping the Allied advance. For two years the German people experienced **'total war'** – every aspect of life was devoted to the war effort.	<ul><li>**Bombing** increased as the Allies tried to destroy the morale of German civilians. The raids caused homelessness and death on a huge scale. In Hamburg in July 1943, 45,000 people died.</li><li>All professional **sport** was stopped.</li><li>No non-military clothes were produced – instead centres opened where people could swap their **clothes**.</li><li>**Sweetshops** were closed.</li><li>Some **foods** were no longer available.</li><li>The regime kept up a barage of propaganda to keep German support strong.</li></ul>
July 1944–May 1945: Defeat	
By July 1944, it was clear Germany was going to **lose the war**. Allied forces were advancing into Eastern and Western Europe. **Refugees** were pouring into Germany. Many features of the proud and well-organised Nazi state were collapsing.	<ul><li>**Air raids** by the Allies were even more extreme: on two nights in February 1945, approximately 150,000 people were killed in Dresden.</li><li>The Nazi **administration** could not cope, ration cards were no longer honoured and people scavenged for food.</li><li>**Railway** and **postal** services were reduced. Letter boxes were closed.</li><li>**Theatres** and **concert halls** closed (**cinemas** remained open).</li><li>The **Home Guard** was formed.</li><li>All **non-Germans** in Germany had to work in armament factories.</li><li>More **women** were made to work.</li></ul>
In May 1945 the Russians reached Berlin and Nazism was **finished**. Hitler and some of his Nazi ministers committed suicide.	

The Holocaust

The coming of war had a deadly effect on Jews and other minorities. As Germany invaded countries like Poland and the USSR, 6 million Jews came under German control. The Nazis had persecuted Jews before the war, but during the war they used violent methods with the aim of exterminating all Jews.

The Einsatzgruppen: As the German army invaded countries, special SS squads called 'Einsatzgruppen' would follow behind them. Once the area was under their control, these squads would round up Jews in each town, take them into the country and make them dig a trench. They would then line up the Jews in front of this trench and shoot them so that they would fall in. The trench then became a mass grave.

The ghettos: When the German armies invaded cities in Poland, Czechoslovakia and Lithuania, any Jews in the cities were moved into special areas called ghettos. These were shut off from the rest of the city, surrounded by walls, and were overcrowded with people. Water, food and power were cut off and hundreds of Jews died there every day. Anyone who tried to leave the ghetto was shot dead.

The Final Solution: On 31 July 1941 the order came from Goering (the Economics Minister) to Himmler (the Head of the SS) to carry out the *'final solution to the Jewish question in Europe'*. They saw the methods of the Einsatzgruppen and the use of ghettos as inefficient ways of killing Jews. Instead they created special death camps which were aimed at killing people, rather than imprisoning them.

By the end of the war, 6 million Jews had been killed in the death camps, as well as other people the Nazis considered 'undesirable': Gypsies, homosexuals and 4 million Russian prisoners of war.

Examiner's tip

You won't get questions in an exam about the detail of military events in the Second World War but you need to know the key phases to understand the changing impact on Germany.

Revision task

The most likely questions in the exam will be about how the war affected each of the groups you have been studying in this topic:

- young people
- women
- minorities
- workers.

For each group find two examples of how life changed for them as a result of the war.

Exam practice

1. Study Source A (on page 124). What is the message of this poster? **[7]**

2. Briefly describe how the Nazis reduced unemployment after 1933. **[5]**

3. Explain why some young people opposed the Nazis. **[7]**

4. 'Nazi policy towards women was confused.' Explain how far you agree with this statement. **[9]**

Answers online

Examiner's tip

For question 1 refer to page 35 for advice on source-based questions. Think back to what you know about Nazi anti-Semitic policies (see page 124).

For question 3 you can use these steps to plan your answer:

- What did Hitler do that affected young people?
- Why would some young people oppose this?
- Include a specific example, such as the Edelweiss Pirates or the White Rose.

For question 4 make sure you consider the way that the pressures of war undermined some of the Nazi policies.